D0790143

Beyond Technology

Questioning, Research and the Information Literate School

by Jamie McKenzie

FNO Press
Bellingham, Washington
Order copies online at
http://fnopress.com

FNO Press　　　　　http://fnopress.com

This work contains many articles previously published in a number of journals and publications. They have all been rewritten and updated for this volume.

"The Research Cycle" first appeared in the June, 1995 issue of **Multimedia Schools**.

" Planning the Voyage," "The Hunt," "More Hunting," "Needles from Haystacks," "Regrouping Findings," and "Information to Persuasion" all appeared as a series in the September, 1995 to February, 1996 issues of **Technology Connection**.

"The Information Literate School Community" first appeared in the March, 1999 issue of **Connected Classroom**.

"Acing the Standards" first appeared in the December, 1999 issue of **eSchool News**.

"Questions as Technology," "Research Programs for an Information Age," "Questioning Toolkit," "Students in Resonance," "Telling Questions," "Searching for the Grail," "The New Plagiarism," and "Strategic Teaching" were first published in **From Now On**.

This collection is dedicated
to the many inspiring teachers
who challenged me
to make up my own mind
and to the many others
who have shown me
that questioning may be
the most powerful technology
ever created.

About the author . . .

Jamie McKenzie is the Editor of **From Now On - The Educational Technology Journal**, a Web-based **ZINE** published since 1991 at http://fno.org. In this journal he has argued for information literate schools. More than 25 per cent of his 19,000+ subscribers live in countries outside of the United States such as Australia, New Zealand, Sweden, Malaysia and Singapore.

From 1993-1997, Jamie was the Director of Libraries, Media and Technology for the Bellingham (WA) Public Schools, a district of 18 schools and 10,000 students which was fully networked with 2000 desktops all tied to the Internet in 1994/95. He has now moved on to support information literacy and professional development for schools across North America as well as Australia and New Zealand.

A graduate of Yale with an MA from Columbia and an Ed.D. from Rutgers, Jamie has been a middle school teacher of English and social studies, an assistant principal, an elementary principal, an assistant superintendent in Princeton (NJ) and a superintendent of two districts on the East coast of the U.S. He also taught four-year-olds in Sunday school.

Jamie has published and spoken extensively on the introduction of new information technologies to schools. In recent times he has paid particular attention to information literacy and how it may transform classrooms and schools to support student centered, engaged learning.

A full resume listing publication credits and a detailed career history is available online at http://fno.org/resume.html.

Introduction

We must move past the current preoccupation with wires, networks and computers. We must move beyond technology for the sake of technology. **IT** (Information Technology) does not transform schools (by **IT**self).

Great teaching combined with information literacy and questioning skills might transform schools, but there has been entirely too much focus on the promise of wires and cables, laptops and desktops. There has been far too much spending on equipment and too little on professional development and program development.

Five years into this global "PC rush," we have scanty evidence that the huge expenditures have improved student performance. Politicians wax eloquent about "knowledge economies" while squandering money on poorly conceived educational ventures that ignore what we know about teachers, teaching and change in schools.

It is time we replace the term **IT** (Information Technology) with **IL** (Information Literacy). **IT** is mainly about flow - the movement of information through networks of various kinds. But adding information in a time of infoglut and data smog (Shenk, 1998) can actually interfere with learning and understanding. Information abundance can overwhelm and drown the learner in irrelevant and unreliable information.

IL is mainly about developing understanding and insight. Literacy is about interpretation of information to guide decisions, solve problems and steer through uncertain, complex futures.

What we need most now is a commitment to **IL** by schools as they strive to improve the reading, writing and thinking of their students.

Introduction

This will entail a sincere and robust commitment to professional development to help the current generation of teachers learn how to use the new electronic tools in ways that count.

This book, along with its companion, **How Teachers Learn Technology Best** (FNO Press, 1999) outlines the considerable investment in program development required for schools to make **IL** central to purpose. **Problems of Readiness and Preparation,** The September, 1999 report of Market Data Retrieval claims that more than 60% of the teachers replying to a survey indicated that they were not well prepared to use these technologies in their classrooms.

NOTE: Because this book is a collection of previously published articles, the reader will sometimes note that basic themes and some content is repeated across some of the chapters. The author has made some attempt to reduce redundancy by rewriting and winnowing the original articles. At the same time, some elements remain important within chapters such as those devoted to the **Research Cycle**. Chapter Eight provides an overview. The following six chapters provide an elaboration. Some repetition was unavoidable.

Contents

Part One

The Primacy of Questioning

Chapter 1 - Questions as Technology

*Questions and questioning may be
the most powerful technologies of all.*

How might this be so?

Questions allow us to make sense of the world. They are the most powerful tools we have for making decisions and solving problems, for inventing, changing and improving our lives as well as the lives of others.

Questioning is central to learning and growing. An unquestioning mind is one condemned to "feeding" on the ideas and solutions of others. An unquestioning mind may have little defense against the data smog so typical of life in this Information Age. An unquestioning mind is like a sloop without a rudder swept along with the tides.

In a democratic society, questions empower citizens to challenge and steer authority to do the most good for the most people.

In a fascist society, questions and questioning are viewed with suspicion. They are discouraged unless they stay within "safe" zones such as science and technology. In the popular children's story, Harry Potter is denied the right to ask questions by his foster parents.

Questions enable us to make changes in life, to invent new and better ways of doing things. They are the "mindware" that enable us to weigh the value of the other tools, determining the best uses for computers, networks, databases and media.

Life is such a puzzle - all those fragments confounding us with thousands of pieces of some huge jigsaw laid out across the oaken table of a summer cottage. Each day we return to the table. We struggle to move the pieces around until some picture emerges, until we discover a pattern or a trend, until we can make sense of nonsense. We wrestle with the information flow and flux. We squint. We frown. We dig. We probe. We sift and sort. We reach into our questioning toolkit and find the right net or lasso or scalpel to bring us closer to some Truth that may serve us well.

> *The scientific mind does not so much provide*
> *the right answers as ask the right questions.*
> Claude Lévi-Strauss

Because the new information landscape is streaming by us at supersonic speeds, we find ourselves working overtime to "get our minds around" the essential issues, trends and data of our times. Making meaning is harder than ever before. Quick fixes, wizards and templates abound as substitutes for deeper understanding, but the ultimate answer to information abundance and degradation is powerful thinking. The better we are at interpreting the data and challenging the assumptions behind them, the greater our chances of handling the riddles, the conundrums and the paradoxes that are so prevalent.

Supersonic speeds? We open our e-mail and watch a stream of messages flow into out mailboxes, some of them correspondence, some of them spam and many of them information "alerts" we have set in motion by subscribing to many of the services that may be tailored to our interests and needs. It is hard to keep up with this torrent.

Questions as Technology

Coping with Info-Glut and Charlatans

When we turn to our desktops for information, we often find millions of documents within a single "mouseclick." Are they worth reading? Will they satisfy our curiosity? Cast light on our biggest concerns?

Looking for financial projections? We uncover thousands. Many are by amateurs and those of questionable credentials. Many predictions contradict the augury of others. Divination is widely practiced but poorly supervised. The Greeks may have done better with their omens, with their seers, prophets and soothsayers, but we must "suffer fools" and wade through the fortune telling and visioning of prophets who are unlicensed and unschooled.

How do we sort and sift our way past the charlatans and self anointed frauds of this new electronic marketplace? How do we protect ourselves from the deceitful? For those who work in schools, how do we raise young people capable of finding their way through this maze?

Powerful questioning is the answer.

Powerful questioning leads to Information Power - the ability to fashion solutions, decisions and plans that are original, cogent and effective.

When we come to a Web page or online article, we immediately ask who put it there and whether their ideas can be trusted. We might also challenge the author of a book. What is their background? their experience? their bias? their funding? their track record? their reputation?

None of us can be expert in everything. We must rely to some extent upon others to help us interpret the world, but we must also be wary of "experts" lacking in wisdom, discretion or reliability. We cannot take the time to conduct original, primary source research each time we look for good ideas. We must turn to the sages.

Prior to the Internet, "experts" usually had to pay dues and win various licenses or credentials. It was difficult to win "air time" without passing through some kind of scrutiny or review.

3

Questions as Technology

The Internet has made the life of charlatans much easier. We find Web sites proudly dispensing hogwash and blather of the worst kind - history that isn't history and medicine that isn't medicine. We open e-mail "stock tips" from spammers who are paid to recommend securities. We visit search engines and directories that spotlight information that has paid for "shelf space." In the 1950s, this was called "payola" and thought of as bribery. At the turn of this century it is a simple fact of e-commerce that advice is often tainted by conflicts of interests and inappropriate partnerships.

> *We never stop investigating. We are*
> *never satisfied that we know enough to*
> *get by. Every question we answer leads*
> *on to another question. This has become*
> *the greatest survival trick of our species.*
>
> Desmond Morris

Matters of Definition

Why have we allowed vendors and merchants to misappropriate the word "technology," applying it primarily to tools that plug into the wall and operate on electrical power? Why do we create a special subject area in schools separate from the real classrooms and call it "technology?" Why do we set up skills lists, tests and outcome statements that encourage the use of electronic tools apart from curriculum content?

> *In the animal kingdom, the rule is, eat or*
> *be eaten; in the human kingdom, define*
> *or be defined.*
>
> Thomas Szasz

How can anyone justify spreadsheeting divorced from real questions as a worthwhile endeavor? or PowerPointing? or Internetting?

Yet we see this trendy approach to information and to learning sweeping through schools and towns with little opposition or concern. Being good at technology, we are assured, is crucial if we wish a comfortable future for our children.

Definitions help to sell product. They carve out territory. They help to establish turf. They focus the spotlight. They shape budgets and priorities.

Matters of Priority and Quality

Even though print books are technologies - information delivery systems with distinct advantages over some of their new, electronic relatives - they have been pushed aside in some places (along with libraries and librarians) by the information Gold Rush and they have been relegated to basement status. Even though much of the new information is of inferior quality, the glitz, the glamour, the ratings and the profits go to the electronic sources.

Traditional publishers such as **Encyclopedia Britannica** may be threatened with extinction, according to a 1999 **New York Times** article, ("Encyclopedia Green; The High Road at a High Cost.," by Edward Wyatt, October 24, 1999) as they find the online world and software companies offering electronic encyclopedias of far lesser scholarship at bargain (often bundled) rates. The creation of scholarly encyclopedias is costly and unlikely to continue, according to this article, as the commoditization of information moves forward relentlessly.

Families too often find the cheaper, substandard, bundled encyclopedia articles quite sufficient for most school reports and family questions. Mind bytes and mind candy abound as the lives of presidents, poets and revolutionaries are reduced to simple paragraphs and formulaic summaries.

Questions as Technology

Simple Answers to Complex Questions

In all too many cases, the questioning process has been reduced and oversimplified to a search for prepackaged answers. Artificial intelligence abounds.

Questions are intended to provoke thought and inspire reflection, but all too often the process is short circuited by the simple answer, the quick truth or the appealing placebo.

We know that the most important questions in life defy such formulaic responses and that recipe books require frequent revision in times of rapid change. Strong questioning skills fuel and steer the inventive process required to "cook up" something new. Without such skills, we and our students are prisoners of conventional wisdom and the trend or bandwagon of the day.

Synthesis - the development of new possibilities by modifying and rearranging elements - cannot be managed without analysis, the probing questioning process that explores the underlying principles, characteristics and possibilities of any given situation. Analysis is the underpinning of new thinking and wise choices.

If we hope to see inventive thought infused with critical judgment, questions and questioning must become a priority of schooling and must gain recognition as a supremely important technology. We must lay aside the forked branches of earlier times, the divining rods of soothsayers, technologists and futurists. Rather than reading the entrails or taking the omens to determine the future, we wield powerful questions as tools to construct a future of our own choosing.

Chapter 2 - Research for an Information Age

Once you have learned how to ask relevant and appropriate questions, you have learned how to learn and no one can keep you from learning whatever you want or need to know.
Neil Postman and Charles Weingartner
Teaching as a Subversive Activity

Smart questions are essential technology for those who venture onto the Information Highway.

Without strong questioning skills, you are just a passenger on someone else's tour bus. You may be on the highway, but someone else is doing the driving.

Without strong questioning skills, you are unlikely to exercise profitable search strategies that allow you to cut past the Info-Glut Info-Garbage and Info-Glitz that all too often impede the search for Insight.

Sometimes this new information landscape seems more like Eliot's Wasteland than a library, more like a yard sale than a gold mine. The weaker the questioning and learning skills, the less value one is likely to discover or uncover.

Schools without a strong commitment to student questioning and research are wasting their money if they install expensive networks linking classrooms to rich electronic information resources.

As long as schools are primarily about teaching rather than learning, there is little need for expanded information capabilities. Considering the reality that schools and publishers have spent decades compressing and compacting human knowledge into efficient packages and delivery systems like textbooks and lectures, they may not be prepared for this new information landscape that calls for independent thinking, exploration, invention and intuitive navigation.

If districts do not commit as much as 25 per cent of their hardware expenditures to curriculum revision and staff development with a focus upon student questioning and research, they are likely to suffer from the Screensaver Disease.*

*We are talking about the educational equivalent of educational Red Ink - the observable failure of schools to actually use their expensive network or computers to any meaningful extent because they are not seen as part of the school's primary mission. In all too many places that mission is defined primarily in terms of covering the curriculum (rapidly) and preparing students to score well on various state tests.

Prime Questions

Which questions matter?

Most important thinking requires one of these three Prime Questions:

1. Why?

Why do things happen the way they do?

This question requires analysis of cause-and-effect and the relationship between variables. It leads naturally to problem-solving (the How question) or to decision-making (the Which is best? question.)

Why? is the favorite question of four-year-olds.

It is the basic tool for figuring stuff out (constructivist learning.)

At one point while researching student questions in one school district, I found **Why?** occurred most often in kindergarten classrooms and least often in the high school (which had the highest SAT scores in the state.)

Why does the sun fall each day? Why does the rain fall?
Why do some people throw garbage out their car windows?
Why do some people steal?
Why do some people treat their children badly?

Research Programs

Why can't I ask more questions in school?

2. How?

How could things be made better?

This question is the basis for problem-solving and synthesis.

Using questions to pull and change things around until a new, better version emerges.

How? is the inventor's favorite question.

How is the tool that fixes the broken furnace and changes the way we get cash from a bank.

How inspires the software folks to keep sending us upgrades and hardware folks to create faster chips.

How is the question that enables the suitor to capture his or her lover's heart.

How is the reformer's passion and the hero's faith.

3. Which?

Which do I select?

This question requires thoughtful decision-making - a reasoned choice based upon explicit (clearly stated) criteria and evidence.

Which? is the most important question of all because it determines who we become. **Which** school or trade will I pick for myself? **Which** path will I follow?

TWO roads diverged in a yellow wood,
And sorry I could not travel both
And be one traveler, long I stood
> Robert Frost

Faced with a moral dilemma, **Which** path will I follow? Confronted by a serious illness, **Which** treatment will I choose for myself?

What happens in most schools?

There have always been plenty of questions in schools, but most of them have come from the teacher, often at the rate of one question every 2-3 seconds.

Unfortunately, these rapid fire questions are not the questions we need to encourage because they tend to be RECALL questions rather than questions requiring higher level thought.

The most important questions of all are those asked by students as they try to make sense out of data and information. These are the questions that enable students to Make Up Their Own Minds.

Powerful questions - Smart Questions, if you will - are the foundation for Information Power, Engaged Learning and Information Literacy.

Sadly, most studies of classroom exchanges in the past few decades report that student questions have been an endangered species for quite some time. (Goodlad, 1984: Sizer, 1984, Hyman, 1980; etc.)

Information-savvy schools should adopt a basic questioning toolkit and then blend it explicitly into each curriculum area where such skills belong.

A Questioning Toolkit

Each district should create a Questioning Toolkit that contains several dozen kinds of questions and questioning tools. This Questioning Toolkit should be printed in large type on posters that reside on classroom walls close by networked, information-rich computers.

Portions of the Questioning Toolkit should be introduced as early as Kindergarten so that students can bring powerful questioning technologies and techniques with them as they arrive in high school.

The next chapter outlines such a Questioning Toolkit and explores the value or purpose of each question type.

Research Programs

Essential Questions	Subsidiary Questions	Hypothetical Questions	Telling Questions	Planning Questions
Organizing Questions	Probing Questions	Sorting & Sifting Questions	Clarification Questions	Strategic Questions
Elaborating Questions	Unanswerable Questions	Inventive Questions	Provocative Questions	Irrelevant Questions
Divergent Questions	Irreverent Questions	As well as other types useful in the search for meaning.		

A Commitment to a Research Model

Given the reality that most teachers passed through school at a time when the prime approach to research was topical, schools should take a careful look at the half dozen or so research models available to help structure school research to emphasize higher level thinking, problem solving and decision-making.

This book describes the operation of one model, the **Research Cycle,** in Chapters 8-14, and lists several others worth considering.

The Research Cycle

Artwork by Sarah McKenzie and Nico Toutenhoofd
Insight Designs at http://www.insightdesigns.com

Chapter 3 - Questioning Toolkit

What types of questions will equip our students with the ability to make sense of their complex worlds? No one list could possibly identify every type required, in part because a changing world may demand new types of questions to fit new circumstances.

The list offered within this chapter is meant to be a beginning, not a final package. Each school should adopt a model of questioning that matches the age and readiness of its students, keeping in mind that even four year olds can (and often must) wrestle with incredibly demanding questions and issues if they are presented in terms and words that match their age.

Essential Questions	Subsidiary Questions	Hypothetical Questions	Telling Questions	Planning Questions
Organizing Questions	Probing Questions	Sorting & Sifting Questions	Clarification Questions	Strategic Questions
Elaborating Questions	Unanswerable Questions	Inventive Questions	Provocative Questions	Irrelevant Questions
Divergent Questions	Irreverent Questions	As well as other types you find useful in the search for meaning.		

Different types of questions accomplish different tasks and help us to build up our answers in different ways.

We must show our students the features of each type of question so they know which combination to employ with the essential question at hand. We don't want them reaching into their toolkit blindly, grasping the first question that comes to mind.

No sense grabbing a screw driver when a wrench is needed. No use seizing the hammer when a saw is required. We want them to reach for the question that matches the job.

Essential Questions

These are questions that touch our hearts and souls. They are central to our lives. They help to define what it means to be human. Most important thought during our lives will center on such Essential Questions.

- What does it mean to be a good friend?
- What kind of friend shall I be?
- Who will I include in my circle of friends?
- How shall I treat my friends?
- How do I cope with the loss of a friend?
- What can I learn about friends and friendships from the novels we read in school?
- How can I be a better friend?

When we draw a cluster diagram of the Questioning Toolkit (opposite page) Essential Questions stand at the center of all the other types of questions. All the other questions and questioning skills serve the purpose of "casting light upon" or illuminating Essential Questions.

Most Essential Questions are interdisciplinary in nature. They cut across the lines created by schools and scholars to mark the terrain of departments and disciplines. Essential Questions probe the deepest issues confronting us - complex and baffling matters that elude simple answers:

Life - Death - Marriage - Identity - Purpose - Betrayal - Honor - Integrity - Courage - Temptation - Faith - Leadership - Addiction - Invention - Inspiration.

The greatest novels, the greatest plays, the greatest songs and the

Questioning Toolkit

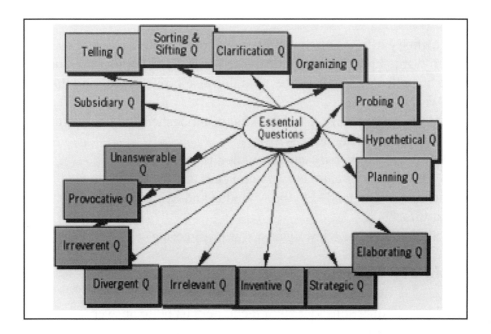

greatest paintings all explore Essential Questions in some manner. Essential Questions are at the heart of the search for Truth.

Many of us believe that schools should devote more time to Essential Questions and less time to Trivial Pursuit. One major reform effort, the Coalition of Essential Schools, has made Essential Questions a keystone of its learning strategy.

Essential Questions offer the organizing focus for a unit. If the U.S. History class will spend a month on a topic such as the Civil War, students explore the events and the experience with a mind toward casting light upon one of the following questions, or they develop Essential Questions of their own.

• Why do we have to fight wars?

• Do we have to fight wars?

• How could political issues or ideas ever become more important than family loyalties?

• Some say our country remains wounded by the slavery experience and the Civil War. In what ways might this claim be true and in what ways untrue? What evidence might substantiate your case?

Questioning Toolkit

• Military officers often complain that the effective conduct of modern war is impeded by political interference and popular pressures on the home front. To what extent did this also prove true during the Civil War?

• How can countries avoid the kind of bloodshed and devastation we experienced during our Civil War?

• How much diversity can any nation tolerate?

• Who showed greater bravery and courage, the front line soldiers and the nurses who tended to the wounded and dying or the leaders of the war effort?

• Should there be a law against war profiteering?

Subsidiary questions

These are questions that combine to help us build answers to our Essential Questions. Big questions spawn families of smaller questions that lead to insight.

The more skillful we and our students become at formulating and then categorizing subsidiary questions, the more success we will have constructing new knowledge.

All of the question categories listed and explained below are types of subsidiary questions. We have several strategies from which to choose when developing a comprehensive list of subsidiary questions for our project:

• We can brainstorm and list every question that comes to mind, utilizing a huge sheet of paper or a word processing program or a graphical organizing program such as Inspiration (http://www.inspiration.com), putting down the questions as they "come to mind." Later we can move these around until they end up along side of related questions. This movement is one advantage of software. This approach has the benefit of spontaneity.

• We can take a list of question categories like the one outlined in this article and generate questions for each category. This approach helps provoke thought and questions in categories that we might not otherwise consider.

In the (condensed) illustration below, a team is pondering the following Essential Question: What is the best way for our school to involve students in the use of e-mail? They begin by listing every question they can think up. They have one member type the list into the outlining part of Inspiration. They could use a word processor instead, but Inspiration will automatically convert their outline into a variety of diagrams and will allow them to move questions around later.

Best way to involve students in the use of e-mail?
- Worst that can happen?
- Potential benefits?
- Obstacles that must be overcome?
- Available resources? Sufficient resources? Additional resources?
- Good models?
- How prepare students? How prepare parents?
- Relationship to discipline code?
- Timing?
- Who does what?
- Assessing progress?

This outline is transformed in seconds by a simple mouseclick into this cluster diagram.

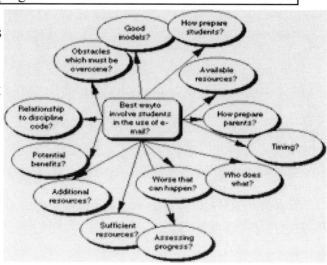

Questioning Toolkit

The lack of order and logic should be immediately visible. This diagram needs to be redrawn. No problem. Point. Click. Drag!

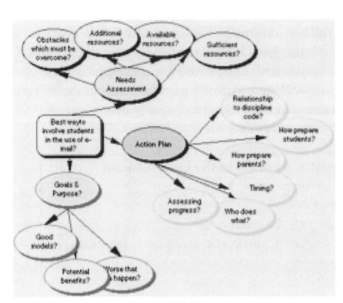

In just 4-5 minutes, we have a cluster diagram that groups questions.

Hypothetical Questions

These are questions designed to explore possibilities and test relationships. They usually project a theory or an option out into the future, wondering what might happen if.

Suppose the earth had no moon. What if the South had won the Civil War?

Hypothetical Questions are especially helpful when trying to decide between a number of choices or when trying to solve a problem.

When we began to generate questions that would help us decide whether or not to offer e-mail accounts to our students, we asked . .

What's the worst that might happen? What are the potential benefits?

Hypothetical Questions are especially useful when we want to see if our hunches, our suppositions and our hypotheses have any merit.

Telling Questions

Telling Questions lead us (like a smart bomb) right to the target. They are built with such precision that they provide sorting and sifting during the gathering or discovery process. They focus the investigation so that we gather only the very specific evidence and information we require, only those facts that cast light upon or illuminate the main question at hand.

In schools that give students e-mail accounts, what is the rate of suspension for abusing the privilege? In schools that give students e-mail accounts, what percentage of students lose their privilege during each of the first ten months? second ten months?

The better the list of telling questions generated by the researcher, the more efficient and pointed the subsequent searching and gathering process. A search strategy may be profoundly shifted by the development of telling questions.

As you can see below - students trying to rank the relative safety of ten cities in the Heartland will have greater success with their search if they translate their general question about crime (Which city is safest?) into a Telling Question (What is the violent crime rate for cities in New England as reported by the Federal Bureau of Justice and how has it changed over the past ten years?).

This would tend to be true whether they were searching on the free Internet or using an electronic encyclopedia or a pay-for-service collection of new articles. The addition of precise elements to a search can radically reduce wasteful wandering.

Search for General Question
crime AND cities AND "Midwest"

Search for Telling Question
"Bureau of Justice" AND statistics AND homicides

Questioning Toolkit

Planning Questions

Planning Questions lift us above the action of the moment and require that we think about how we will structure our search, where we will look and what resources we might use such as time and information. If we were sailing West on a square masted ship, we would pass off the wheel and the lines to teammates in order to climb to the crow's nest - a lofty perch from which we could look over the horizon.

Too many researchers, be they student or adult, make the mistake of burying their noses in their studies and their sources. They have trouble seeing the forest, so close do they stand to the pine needles. They are easily lost in a thicket of possibilities.

The effective researcher develops a plan of action in response to Planning Questions like these:

Sources
• Who has done the best work on this subject?
• Which group may have gathered the best information?
• Which medium (Internet, CD-ROM, electronic periodical collection, scholarly book, etc.) is likely to provide the most reliable and relevant information with optimal efficiency?
• Which search tool or index will speed the discovery process?

Sequence
• What are all of the tasks that need completing in order to generate a credible product that offers fresh thought backed by solid evidence and sound thinking?
• What is the best way to organize these tasks over time? How much time is available? Which tasks come first, and then?
• Which tasks depend upon others or cannot be completed until others are finished?

Pacing
• How much time is available for this project?
• How long does it take to complete each of the tasks required?

Questioning Toolkit

- How much time can be applied to each task?
- Do some tasks require more care and attention than others?
- Can some tasks be rushed?
- Is it possible to complete the project in the time available?
- How should the plan be changed to match the time resources?

Organizing Questions

Organizing Questions make it possible to structure our findings into categories that will allow us to construct meaning. Without these structures we suffer from hodge podge and mish mash - information collections akin to trash heaps and landfills, large in mass, lacking in meaning. The less structure we create in the beginning, the harder it becomes later to find patterns and relationships in the fragments or the collection of bits and pieces.

If we are trying to compare and contrast three cities (or three products or three bills or three artists) we might use our criteria and our telling questions as the basis for the fields and the entries in our database. Or we may develop a word processing file around these criteria and questions that becomes the collecting mechanism for our findings.

Cities Database

Source:
Subject:
Keywords:
Abstract:

Questioning Toolkit

Each time we come upon valuable findings, we extract the relevant data and place them where they belong. If we find facts about the violent crime rate in Portland, for example, we enter them along with their source as a record in the database that might look something like this:

Cities Database

Source: Money Online: Best Places: Money ranks the
300 biggest places - URL: http://www.pathfinder.com/
Subject words: Portland Crime
Keywords: violent crime rate
Abstract: 270.5 crimes per 100,000 people vs. 716
crimes National average

Our challenge is teaching students to paraphrase, condense and then place their findings thoughtfully rather than cutting and pasting huge blocks of text that have been unread, undigested and undistilled.

Probing Questions

Probing Questions take us below the surface to the heart of the matter. They operate somewhat like the archeologist's tools - the brushes that clear away the surface dust and the knives that cut through the accumulated grime and debris to reveal the outlines and ridges of some treasure. Another appropriate metaphor might be exploratory surgery.

The good doctor spends little time on the surface, knowing full well that the vital organs reside at a deeper level.

We never stop investigating. We are never satisfied that we know enough to get by.

tion. This has become the greatest survival trick of our species.
Desmond Morris

The search for insight involves some of the same exploratory elements. We look for the same kind of "convergence" that guides oil prospecting. The geologist knows that the odds of finding oil are greatly increased when three or four elements are all present in the same location.

When it comes to information-seeking, the convergence is established by creating a logical intersection of search words and key concepts, the combination of which is most likely to identify relevant sites and articles.

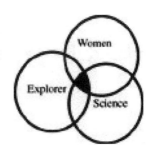

Probing Questions allow us to push search strategies well beyond the broad topical search to something far more pointed and powerful.

And when we first encounter an information "site," we rarely find the treasures lying out in the open within easy reach. We may need to "feel for the vein" much as the lab technician tests before drawing blood. This "feeling" is part logic, part prior knowledge, part intuition and part trial-and-error.

Logic - We check to see if there is any structure to the way the information is organized and displayed, if there are any sign posts or clues pointing to where the best information resides. We assume the author had some plan or design to guide placement of information and we try to identify its outlines.

Prior Knowledge - We apply what we have seen and known in the past to guide our search. We consider information about the topic and prior experience with information sites. This prior knowledge helps us to avoid dead ends and blind alleys. It helps us to make wise choices when browsing through lists of "hits."

Prior knowledge also makes it easier to interpret new findings, to place them into a context and distinguish between "fool's gold" and the real thing.

Intuition - We explore our hunches, follow our instincts, look for patterns and connections, and make those leaps our minds can manage. Especially when we are hoping to create new knowledge and carve out new insights, this non-rational, nonlogical form of information harvesting is critically important.

Trial-and-Error - Sometimes, nothing works better than plain old "mucking about." Push here. Tug there.

Try this out! We find a site with so much information and so little structure that we have little choice but to plunge in and see what we can find.

Sorting & Sifting Questions

Sorting & Sifting Questions enable us to manage Infoglut and Info-Garbage - the hundreds of hits and pages and files that often rise to the surface when we conduct a search - culling and keeping only the information that is pertinent and useful.

Relevancy is the primary criterion employed to determine which pieces of information are saved and which are tossed overboard. We create a "net" of questions that allows all but the most important information to slide away. We then place the good information with the questions it illuminates.

- Which parts of this data are worth keeping?
- Will this information shed light on any of my questions?"
- Is this information reliable?
- How much of this information do I need to place in my database?
- How can I summarize the best information and ideas?
- Are there any especially good quotations to paste in the abstract field?

Questioning Toolkit

Clarification Questions

Clarification Questions convert fog and smog into meaning. A collection of facts and opinions does not always make sense by itself.

Hits do not equal TRUTH. A mountain of information may do more to block understanding than promote it.

Defining words and concepts is central to this clarification process.

- What do they mean by "violent crime rate?" Do they use the same definition and standards as the FBI?
- What do they mean by "declining rate of increase?"
- How did they gather their data? Was it a reliable and valid process? Do they show the data and evidence they claim to have in support of their conclusions? Was is substantial enough to justify their conclusions?
- Did they gather evidence and data?

Examining the coherence and logic of an argument, an article, an essay, an editorial or a presentation is fundamental.

- How did they develop the case they are presenting?
- What is the sequence of ideas and how do they relate one to another?
- Do the ideas logically follow one from the other?

Determining the underlying assumptions is vital.

- How did they get to this point?
- Are there any questionable assumptions below the surface or at the foundation of the argument?

> Clever people seem not to feel the natural pleasure of
> bewilderment, and are always answering questions
> when the chief relish of a life is to go on asking them.
> Frank Moore Colby

Questioning Toolkit

Strategic Questions

Strategic Questions focus on ways to make meaning.

The researcher must switch from tool to tool and strategy to strategy while passing through unfamiliar territory. Closely associated with the planning questions formulated early on in this process, Strategic Questions arise during the actual hunting, gathering, inferring, synthesizing and ongoing questioning process.

- What do I do next?
- How can I best approach this next step?, this next challenge? this next frustration?
- What thinking tool is most apt to help me here?
- What have I done when I've been here before? What worked or didn't work? What have others tried before me?
- What type of question would help me most with this task?
- How do I need to change my research plan?

Elaborating Questions

Elaborating Questions extend and stretch the import of what we are finding. They take the explicit and see where it might lead. They also help us to seek below the surface to implicit (unstated) meanings.

- What does this mean?
- What might it mean if certain conditions and circumstances changed?
- How could I take this farther? What is the logical next step? What is missing? What needs to be filled in?
- Reading between the lines, what does this REALLY mean?
- What are the implied or suggested meanings?

Unanswerable Questions

Unanswerable Questions are the ultimate challenge.

They serve like boundary stones, helping us to know when we have pushed insight to its outer limits. When exploring Essential Questions (most of which are unanswerable in the ultimate sense), we may have to settle for "casting light" upon them.

When wrestling with these Unanswerable Questions, we may never find Truth, but we may illuminate - extend the level of understanding and reduce the intensity of the darkness.

> The real questions are the ones that obtrude upon your consciousness whether you like it or not, the ones that make your mind start vibrating like a jackhammer, the ones that you "come to terms with" only to discover that they are still there.
>
> The real questions refuse to be placated. They barge into your life at the times when it seems most important for them to stay away. They are the questions asked most frequently and answered most inadequately, the ones that reveal their true natures slowly, reluctantly, most often against your will.
>
> Ingrid Bengis

- How will I be remembered?
- How much can anyone resist Fate's will?
- What is the Good Life?
- What is friendship?
- How would life be different if . . .

Students wrestling with Essential Questions must be prepared for the strong likelihood that their questions may be Unanswerable. They must be taught that this reality is perfectly acceptable and is no signal to stop searching and thinking.

Inventive Questions

Inventive Questions turn our findings inside out and upside down.

They distort, modify, adjust, rearrange, alter, twist and turn the bits and pieces we have picked up along the way until we can shout "Aha!" and proclaim the discovery of something brand new.

- How do I make sense of these bits and bytes and pieces?
- What does all this information really mean?
- How can I rearrange what I have gathered so that some picture or new insight emerges?
- What needs to be eliminated or reversed or modified in order to make better sense of my findings?
- What is still missing?
- Can any information be regrouped or combined in ways which help meaning to emerge?
- Can I display this information or data in a way which will cast more light on my essential question?

Provocative Questions

Provocative Questions are meant to push, to challenge and to throw conventional wisdom off balance.

They give free rein to doubt, disbelief and skepticism.

> The best servants of the people, like the best valets,
> must whisper unpleasant truths in the master's ear. It is
> the court fool, not the foolish courtier, whom the king
> can least afford to lose.
> Walter Lippmann

Ancient empires and kingdoms in China often employed a court jester or fool whose job it was to challenge and make fun of policies and ideas and key players surrounding the king or queen. The fool could often get away with a level of questioning that would never have been permitted a "legitimate" member of the council.

On the other hand, the fool might also lose his head if the king or queen took offense. A dangerous occupation!

Closely associated with Divergent Questions and Irreverent Questions, Provocative Questions help provide the basis for satire, parody, and expose whether it be **Gulliver's Travels**, **Alice in Wonderland**, or **Dilbert**.

These plays and stories poke fun at politicians and leaders in ways that help protect us from excessive deference or what is called "spin" today.

In the case of student research, we have probably devoted too little attention to irony, satire and parody as an important element in "open systems," a term that describes responsive (and healthy) political systems as well as organizations of various kinds such as schools and corporations.

When inspired by a desire to understand the Truth, Provocative Questions play a positive role in debunking propaganda, mythologies, hype, bandwagons and the Big Lie.

They help us to remove the "bunk" or "claptrap" and determine if there is any substance worth considering. In a time of what Toffler calls "info-tactics" such questions become an essential tool for any citizen in a democratic society.

In an age of infoglut and info-garbage, we must equip students with questions that enable them to separate out meaning from all the competing variants of BLATHER (quoted here from **Roget's Thesaurus**). . .

> empty talk, idle speeches, sweet nothings, endearments, wind, gas, hot air, vaporing, verbiage, DIFFUSENESS rant, ranting and raving, bombast, fustian, rodomontade BOASTING blether, blather, blah-blah-blah, flimflam guff, hogwash, eyewash, claptrap, poppycock, FABLE humbug

- Where's the beef? content? substance? logic? evidence?
- What is the source? Is the source reliable?
- What's the point? Is there a point?
- Cutting past the noise and the rhetoric, is there any insight,

Questioning Toolkit

knowledge or worthwhile information here?

Irrelevant Questions

Irrelevant Questions take us far afield, distract us and threaten to divert us from the task at hand. And that is their beauty!

Truth almost never appears where we might look logically. The creation of new knowledge almost always requires some wandering off course. The more we cling to coastline, the less apt we are to find the New World. As Melville so dramatically pointed out in **Moby Dick**, the search for Truth requires the courage to venture out and away from the familiar and the known.

> But as in landlessness alone resides the highest truth, shoreless, indefinite as God — so, better is it to perish in that howling infinite, than be ingloriously dashed upon the lee, even if that were safety!

Divergent Questions

Divergent Questions use existing knowledge as a base from which to kick off like a swimmer making a turn. They move more logically from the core of conventional knowledge and experience than irrelevant questions.

They are more carefully planned to explore territory that is adjacent to that which is known or understood.

Trying to find a way to restore water quality in a lake or stream? If we limit our search to successful attempts, we may miss out on the chance to avoid other people's mistakes. Sometimes we learn more by studying the opposite of our main target.

In the same sense, we may want to check out efforts to restore air quality and other tangentially related efforts. We may even explore efforts to reintroduce endangered species to various habitats.

Questioning Toolkit

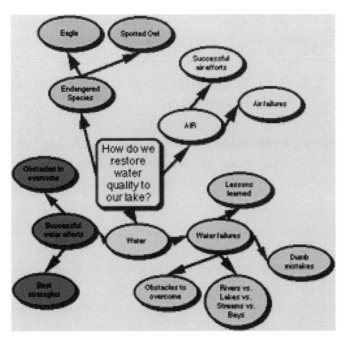

New ideas are rarely sitting waiting for us in obvious places. The ability to freely associate related topics and questions greatly increases the odds that researchers will make important discoveries.

Irreverent Questions

Irreverent Questions explore territory that is "off-limits" or taboo. They challenge far more than conventional wisdom. They hold no respect for authority or institutions or myths. They leap over, under or through walls and rules and regulations.

Socrates found himself in considerable trouble for showing the youth of Athens how to ask Irreverent Questions, and we need to remember that such questions are not universally appreciated. In fact, some folks find such questioning disrespectful and impolite. They question the value of Irreverent Questions.

> It is the human condition to question one god after another, one appearance after another, or better, one apparition after another, always pursuing the truth of

the imagination, which is not the same as the truth of appearance.
    Alain [Émile-Auguste Chartier]

Corporations like IBM have learned that today's heretic - the one with the courage, the tenacity and the brash conviction to question the way things are "spozed to be" - often turns out to be a prophet of sorts. **The Emperor's New Clothes** is the classic story showing what happens when Irreverent Questions are discouraged and obedience, subservience and compliance are prized. The emperor parades naked. The corporation clings blindly to old beliefs.

Chapter 4 - Students in Resonance

Provoking Fresh Thought and Deep Reasoning with Dissonance, Contrast and Juxtaposition

Resonance
-- there is no wisdom without it.
Resonance is a natural phenomenon, the shadow of import alongside the body of fact, and it cannot flourish except in deep time.

Sven Birkerts

How can we be sure our students are doing fresh thinking?

How can we create learning experiences that require deep reasoning and originality?

The answer lies in understanding the interplay between **dissonance, juxtaposition**[2]and **resonance**.

We can employ juxtaposition as a strategy to provoke dissonance.

Students in Resonance

The two photographs above show two very different coffee experiences. They stand side by side in juxtaposition. Their placement is jarring - unsettling. One is immediately tempted to compare and contrast them.

The photographs are available online in color at http://fno.org/oct99/juxtaposition2.html

Two contrasting coffee experiences in Stockholm.

One is warm.	One is cold.
One is asleep.	One is awake.
One is young.	One is old.
One has come a long way.	One is starting out.
One is male.	One is female.
One is poised.	One is resting.
One is ravenous.	One is subdued.
One is bowed.	One is tilting back.

Both are alone.
Both are in the sun.
Both are sitting.

One reads.   One sleeps.
One eats.

Both dream.
People pass by along the street unnoticed.

Students in Resonance

Notice how sharply contrasting images can create dissonance.

We expect that the need to resolve this dissonance will lead to resonance and, ultimately, to insight.

As teachers, we help our students to identify the choices, quandaries and dilemmas embedded in life. They wrestle with the important (essential) questions. They manage irony, paradox and ambiguity.

We give students skills to create meaning where many would find nothing but fog.

When we set two or more ideas, paintings, poems, leaders or cities side by side, we provoke thought and comparison.

idea vs. idea
beach vs. mountain
painting vs. painting
road vs. track
poem vs. poem
leader vs. leader
digital vs. analog
city vs. city
writer vs. writer
freedom vs. license
browser vs. browser
cola vs. cola
cafe vs. cafe
trend vs. fad
bar vs. bistro
investment vs. scheme
proposal vs. proposal
suitor vs. suitor
Internet stock vs. Fortune 500

When we place them thus in juxtaposition, we set in motion thoughts of difference - cognitive dissonance. The sharper the contrast, the greater the dissonance. We can feel the vibration, the conflict, the discomfort.

Students in Resonance

We are thrown off balance. Our minds are intrigued, our curiosities awakened. We want to resolve the dissonance, bring things back into harmony or resonance.

Too much school research and thought has suffered from a singular focus. Topical research (Go find out about California!) lacks the energy and excitement of comparison and choice.

Which city should we move to?

Which job shall we take?

Which neighborhood will make us happy?

Which roommate will endure beyond the first month?

Dissonance and Juxtaposition in ART

The vast digital resources available on the Internet provide countless opportunities to inspire original thought. Examples of dissonance and juxtaposition can be found within images. And images may also be placed side by side to set up the juxtaposition.

Within Images

How do dissonance and juxtaposition add to the meaning and impact of each of these paintings?

Students in Resonance

Comparing Images

Which of these Goyas available at the **Thinker** - The Fine Arts Museums of San Francisco - better shows courage? Go to the **Thinker** at http://www.thinker.org/imagebase/index-2.html to search for a list of Goya "COURAGE" images. Enter "Goya" and "courage" in the Search box midway down the page.

Choices provoke dissonance

Which of these jobs would you prefer if you were living in Victoria in 1890 - 1930? Why?

Coal Mining?
Gold Mining?
Fishing?
Farming?

Explore the digital resources available from Museum Victoria to make your choice. The Biggest Family Album in Australia.
http://pioneer.mov.vic.gov.au/cgi-bin/texhtml?Multimedia

Which of these jobs would you prefer if you were living in the States in 1890 - 1930? Why?

Coal Mining?
Gold Mining?
Fishing?
Farming?

Explore the digital resources available from The Library of Congress to make your choice.
http://memory.loc.gov/ammem/detroit/dethome.html

Students in Resonance

Dissonance and Juxtaposition in Poetry

What examples of dissonance and
juxtaposition can you identify
within the poem below?

Benched

In the third quarter
Before their time
They sit with crossed hands
Watching the game
The fast breaks
Dribbles behind the back
And hook shots

They feed pigeons
Read the paper
Compare grandchildren
And ignore the ghetto blaster
The couple in love

Their eyes shift back and forth
Following the play
Up and down the court
Judging every move
The back door play
Charging violation
And ensuing foul shots
Missed
Careening off the rim

They await the final whistle
Of the final game
The hot shower
The long ride home

Poem and sketch
© by Jamie McKenzie

They sit quietly
Not wanting back in
Knowing the score
Now
Afraid they've lost the touch

Dissonance and Juxtaposition in Datasets

Huge datasets such as this one from the U.S. Department of

Students in Resonance

Justice listing populations and numbers of homicides for the largest American cities are jammed full of comparisons just waiting to be explored. Any time we put information in grids we are juxtaposing information - setting up a comparison.

Which city had the worst homicide rate in 1985?
Which city has the fastest rate of decline in its homicide rate today?
Which regions of the country are most dangerous?

City	Population 1985	Homicides 1985
New York, NY	7,183,984	1384
Los Angeles, CA	3,186,459	777
San Diego, CA	988,284	96
Phoenix, AZ	890,746	89
Dallas, TX	997,467	301
San Antonio, TX	862,878	180
Honolulu, HI	817,083	36
San Jose, CA	706,062	55
Las Vegas MPD Juris	456,749	57
San Francisco, CA	733,456	85
Baltimore, MD	771,097	213
Jacksonville, FL	601,007	90
Columbus, OH	565,682	72
Memphis, TN	654,626	122
Milwaukee, WI	621,931	68
El Paso, TX	474,870	22
Washington, D.C.	626,000	147
Boston, MA	573,131	87
Charlotte-Mecklenbu	335,690	56
Seattle, WA	495,190	61

Source: http://www.usdoj.gov/

Students in Resonance

Stilling the Narrative Voice: Explanation and Explication as Enemies of Thought

We must still the narrative voice, at least part of the time.

The voice at the front of the room.

The voice on the museum's guided tour cassette (unless we welcome the explanations).

The labels next to the paintings. The **Cliff Notes**. The sound bites. The mind bytes. The eye candy and mind candy.

When we explain everything to young people, they do not learn how to interpret for themselves. They yawn. They memorize. They yawn some more. They take notes. They daydream. They yawn. But how much do they remember? Are they growing mentally strong and independent or flabby and dependent upon others to do their thinking for them?

Those of us hoping to enhance the thinking skills of students often focus on the importance of teachers learning to pass back and forth through a spectrum of teaching styles that range from "sage on the stage" to "guide on the aide." It is unlikely that students will learn to make up their own minds or think for themselves if someone stands at the front of the room day after day explaining life, content and curriculum to them.

We have growing evidence that "traditional" teachers (as defined by Hank Becker) are much less likely than "constructivist" teachers to allow students to make frequent and meaningful use of information technologies. Concern about curriculum standards keeps many of these earnest professionals in the role of information provider and wisdom dispenser. Students in such classrooms are restricted to consumption of insight rather than construction of insight. They consume a steady diet of secondary sources and other people's interpretations. They are raised on the educational equivalent of fast food.

We must still the narrative voice, at least part of the time. We must construct information challenges for our students that put them in the roles of Sherlock Holmes and Nancy Drew.

Chapter 5 - Questions and the Information Literate School Community

Networking is not a sufficient goal in itself, as most wired schools quickly learn. This effort is about enhanced performance - students who can write, think, reason and communicate more powerfully. If we follow installation with the right kinds of programs and professional development, we should see smarter, more capable students emerge. We should see young people who can solve problems and make up their own minds.

Looking for a clear focus and a clear purpose? Turn your school into an **information literate school community** and count the blessings.

Professional development programs might well make **information literacy** the centerpiece of all adult learning. If all teachers could develop their own information literacy, they might also turn about and nurture the same skills in their students.

Defining Information Literacy

Information literacy has three major components, all of which require that learners "make up their own minds." Mere gathering of information is old-fashioned and obsolete. We expect inventive thinking from students.

1. **Prospecting**: The first component of information literacy relates to the discovery of pertinent and reliable information. Prospecting requires navigation skills

as well as the ability to sort, sift and select relevant data.

2. **Interpreting**: It is not enough to locate numbers, text and visual data. The learner must be able to translate data and information into knowledge, insight and understanding. The learner must be skilled at interpretation.

3. **Creating Good New Ideas**: True information literacy includes the development of new insights. We must not be satisfied with rehashing the ideas of others. We expect more than thinly disguised plagiarism. We expect good ideas.

It may take three or more years for a school to approach the goal of universal information literacy. The journey requires a substantial and sustained commitment to professional development and program development.

Signs of Progress

How does a school know when it has achieved the status of an information literate school community? When the following characteristics are abundantly evident, the phrase is well deserved. Download the form at (http://fno.org/sept98/traits.doc) for self rating.

• Invention

Much of the school program (25 or more per cent?) is dedicated to problem-solving, decision-making, exploration and the creation of new ideas. Both teachers and students are increasingly engaged in the discovery and building of meaning around challenging questions drawn from the curriculum.

• Fluency

Teachers move back and forth between an array of instructional roles and strategies. Sometimes they are the sage on the stage. Other times they are the guide on the side. They are acquiring an expanding toolkit of strategies.

• Support

The school provides ongoing support for all learners to develop thinking and information skills. These opportunities are rich, frequent and embedded in the daily life of the school.

• Navigation

Learners are developing the agility to find their way through the new information landscape with little lost time.

• Searching

Learners apply Boolean Logic. They search with appropriate syntax. They employ powerful search strategies to carve through mountains of information.

• Selection

Learners know how to separate the reliable from the unreliable source. They recognize propaganda, bias and distortion.

• Questioning

Learners know how and when to employ dozens of different types of questions. Some are best to solve a problem. Others help in making a decision.

• Planning

Learners are acquiring planning and organizational skills. They make wise choices from a toolkit of research strategies and resources. They learn when a particular strategy might produce the best results.

• Interpretation

Learners convert primary sources and raw data into information, and then proceed further (beyond information) to insight. They translate, infer and apply what they have gathered to the issue at hand.

• Deep Thinking

Learners combine deep thinking and reading with a wide-ranging search for relevant information. This quest for information is but the prelude to the more important work: solving a problem, creating a new idea, inventing a product or composing a symphony.

• Commitment

All curriculum documents include clear statements regarding the information literacy expectations that are developmentally appropriate for each grade level.

• Family Involvement

Parents have been brought into the literacy circle as full partners so that time at home is well spent by students who have access to books, computers and other information resources such as visits to the zoo or the museum.

Online Resources

Linda Langford, "Information Literacy: A Clarification" in **School Libraries Worldwide**, Volume 4, Number 1.
http://fno.org/oct98/clarify.html

Information Power: Building Partnerships for Learning that includes **the Information Literacy Standards for Student Learning**.
http://www.ala.org/aasl/ip_implementation.html

"Information literate school community" appears as a goal in **Learning for the Future: Developing information Services in Australian Schools** (1993).
http://www.curriculum.edu.au/catalog/catlibr.htm)

Chapter 6 - Acing the Standards

Despite the five billion dollars being spent annually to equip American schools with networks, we have no credible evidence that this huge investment has translated into improved student performance on important learning tasks such as reading, writing and reasoning. We have been lax with regard to assessment and unfocused with regard to program. We have surfed and fiddled and frittered too long. Our students deserve something much more substantial.

Disappointing Early Results

Even some of the best educational research into Internet uses by teachers (Becker, 1999) paints a somewhat sorry picture of how these new tools are being used with students by most teachers.

Becker's data show that even those teachers with access to four or more networked classroom computers were rarely taking full advantage of the student learning opportunities available.

A New Testing Landscape

Many American states as well as Canadian provinces, Australian states, and countries like New Zealand have been radically shifting the nature of test items to require more independent thinking and inferential reasoning. Along with curriculum standards that call for problem-

Acing the Standards

solving and decision-making, we are seeing a dramatic change in testing that requires students to make up their own minds and figure things out for themselves.

Many of these new tests offer fewer multiple choices and expect students to draft their own responses. In many states, the failure rate approaches or exceeds 50 per cent as thousands of students find themselves ill prepared to respond to such challenges.

An Example from Massachusetts

Fourth graders in Massachusetts read a story about a young girl, Anastasia, who brings home a pet and argues with her mother to let her bring the pet inside. The mother resists. Anastasia persists. The mother resists. Anastasia tries again. And so it goes . . .

"What kind of person is Anastasia? Justify your answer with examples and evidence from the story."

This kind of question requires the reasoning skills we associate with the research process. The student must put 2 and 2 together in order to develop and then support a reasonable answer.

The Need for Strategic Reading

Student scores on demanding tests are likely to rise dramatically if we teach them to start with the questions before they read the passage. They can then read the passage strategically, knowing what clues they need to confirm their hypotheses.

In most cases, two of the multiple choice answers can be rejected logically without even reading the passage. We must teach students to begin by discarding these two. Once they have narrowed down the choices to two survivors, they must know that one is a "teaser" put there to trap them and one is correct. Their job is to pose a hypothesis for a right answer and then read just enough of the passage to dispose of the teaser.

Try it on this next question which is a sample item from Virginia.

Acing the Standards

An Example from Virginia

Which two answers can be discarded immediately?
Which of the remaining two seems most plausible?

What is the main idea of this passage?

A. The sculpture of each President's head on Mt. Rushmore is created from plaster models.

B. Borglum planned the final appearance of Mt. Rushmore by rearranging plaster models of the Presidents' heads.

*C. Carving huge likenesses of four Presidents on Mt. Rushmore involved years of hard work on the mountain face.

D. Numbers were painted on the rock of Mt. Rushmore to show the amount of stone that needed to be removed from each part of the Presidents' heads.

When we speak of teaching strategic reading, we expect that students will learn the strategies employed by proficient readers as identified by research into effective reading. **Mosaic of Thought: Teaching Comprehension in a Reader's Workshop** (Keene & Zimmerman, 1997) describes how Colorado teachers have used this approach to strengthen the reading comprehension of elementary students.

Researchers have found that proficient readers - ones with strong comprehension abilities - use their minds quite differently than those who read word by word, sounding out the words without much under-standing of content.

Teachers model each of the strategies one at a time and then give students ample opportunities to practice each strategy until it becomes a habit of mind. Once a reasonable level of mastery has been attained, they move on to the next strategy and devote a month or more to the new one until it, too, is mastered.

Drawing from Mosaic (pp. 22-23) we can derive a strategic approach to challenging reading questions and passages.

Acing the Standards

Questioning

Students begin with the questions rather than the passage, and then they pose more questions about the questions. We build answers to big questions by figuring out the smaller or "subsidiary" questions that point the way to an answer.

In the Mt. Rushmore question above, for example, the student looks at the question:

"What is the main idea of this passage?"

And new questions come to mind.

"Which of these 4 choices look like a main idea?"
"Which look like details?"
"Which answer looks like a 'teaser' or trap?"
"Which answers seem like facts rather than ideas?"
"What's my best hunch for the answer?"
"What clues do I need from the passage to check my hunch?"
"Where should I look for these clues?"

If we provide students with explicit practice of this questioning approach, they then turn to reading passages with far more purpose and skill.

Picturing

We encourage students to think visually and to use all of their senses as they look at the questions and move to the passage.

They bring a picture of Mount Rushmore up into their "mind's eye."
(Picture used with permission of the National

Park Service.
http://www.nps.gov)

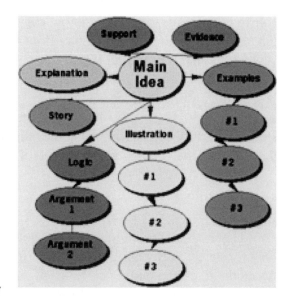

They also look at the passage somewhat like a cluster diagram, wondering how its contents fall into categories.

Instead of starting from the first word of the first paragraph and reading each word and sentence in order from beginning to end, the student browses over the paragraphs and tries to identify the structure. The student looks for "the big picture" and only digs down deeply where the most important information is likely to lie awaiting.

It is no accident that we say, "A picture is worth a thousand words." These visual strategies give us a way or organizing and grasping complexities. They help our students to translate the words into meaning. They convert details and fragments into pictures.

"I get it!" they proclaim, as the main idea comes into focus.

Awakening prior knowledge

Prior knowledge comes in handy right off while discarding obviously wrong answers before turning to read the passage itself. The trick here is to sharpen students' awareness of their substantial knowledge base so they will "dredge up" whatever they know before reading. It may take some intentional searching to bring the data up from storage, but it pays off in better performance.

The technical word used in Mosaic and in reading research is *schema*. If we think of mental scaffolding and the reading task as the construction of meaning, prior knowledge helps to provide the structure upon which to "hang" insight. Prior knowledge provides the context that lends more significance to details and fragments.

Think in terms of jigsaw puzzles. Ever look at the picture on the box before putting the pieces together? Why? The picture helps us to sort and sift the fragments. It works somewhat like that for reading. If students start by considering what they already know and bring it into the reading process, they will be ahead of the game.

Inferring

The most important ideas in the "new" reading tests are not directly stated. They must be inferred - figured out by reading between the lines and putting clues together. The students must play Sherlock Holmes - must be "infotectives" operating on hunches and suppositions, testing hypotheses. Like a good detective, they look for evidence, seek patterns, notice breaks in patterns and manage to dig below the surface to find, create or extend the meaning.

Inference is closely associated with the next strategy and they often work hand-in-hand as the student tries to puzzle things out.

Synthesizing

Synthesis is somewhat like moving the pieces of a jigsaw puzzle around until a picture emerges. It is the thoughtful melding, combining and rearranging of the details, the clues and the elements of a passage until a solid idea or interpretation emerges.

Students who learn to outline their own ideas with a cluster diagramming program like Inspiration may grasp the puzzle metaphor as they "drag" their thoughts and information around on the screen.

The next step is to teach them to outline other writers' thoughts and ideas so they can see the connection between the reading and the writing act - the way that ideas are arranged within passages.

Acing the Standards

Fluency

If at first you don't succeed . . .

The best readers have a trial-and-error spirit that keeps them at the task, making use of every tool and trick in their repertoire until they have some success.

Fluency refers to their ability to move across a menu of strategies until one works. They do not allow themselves to get stuck in one place trying the same wrong tool or strategy over and over again, harder and harder. They are toolmakers and tool-shapers as well as tool-users.

Our job is to equip them with good strategies and also teach them to develop their own.

Four Main Strategies to Enhance Student Performance

This chapter proposes four main ways to employ new technologies to strengthen student reading, writing and thinking:

1. Make Research, Writing & Questioning Central to Schooling

Unless the school makes research, writing and questioning central, the networked technology will be used rarely and tangentially, with a tendency toward special events and trivia rather than bread and butter issues. Rank and file teachers want to see more than virtual field trips and fanciful bike tours of distant continents. They want to see activities that pay off in higher scores and better performance.

The first step is to make research a daily event in every child's life, not just something that happens once a year in February or March when we suddenly devote several weeks to a "state project." Research is the best practice for the kinds of strategic reading discussed earlier.

51

Acing the Standards

The Year Long Project
"Five Hundred Miles"

Each student starts the year by identifying a leader, a celebrity, a crisis, a hobby or some other aspect of life that interests them enough to devote nine months to its study.

Each student becomes an expert on her or his subject and is ultimately expected to convert the expertise into an authentic product.

1. Selection - Each student settles on one field of interest and identifies one particular aspect worthy of tracking.

2. Questioning - Rather than gathering all information regarding the subject, the student will form key questions so that only pertinent information is retained.

3. Storage - This is an opportunity to design an efficient information storage and retrieval system so that the student can sort, sift and interpret even after collecting hundreds of records.

4. Prospecting - Early in the project, the student surveys the information landscape and identifies all relevant, reliable sites. If possible, the student sets up an automated flow (push technology).

5. Monitoring - The student keeps an eye on daily and weekly developments, periodically visiting sites that have expanding resources but no "alert" capability. The student frequently updates sources as new ones emerge or old ones fold.

6. Responding to inquiries - The student has a chance to demonstrate expertise by responding to questions from peers and others either personally or through e-mail.

7. Creating a product - The student shares insight by developing a product of some kind related to the subject. The product should require original thought, data compression and synthesis.

For a full description of how to manage such projects, enjoy the online professional development unit at **500 Miles: The Workshop**. http://fno.org/500miles/persistence.html

Acing the Standards

Essential Questions in Every Unit

Each time a teacher introduces a new unit, the class is shown five or more essential questions and asked to explore one of them during the unit or build one of her or his own (subject to teacher approval).

The Daily Research Question

Each day begins with students walking into the classroom to note an intriguing research question on the board. Puzzles, riddles and curious questions that can be answered reasonably well without months of study. These should require some thought and ingenuity, not be mere trivial pursuit. They should be highly motivating and captivating.

Every Student Skilled at Questioning

To be a successful thinker, reader and writer, each student must possess a Questioning Toolkit - a set of questioning strategies that will support the kinds of reading for meaning outlined earlier. Infotectives have highly developed repertoires of questioning skills.

We teach our students to make effective use of all the question types outlined in Chapter Three.

Ideally, we would hope to see students develop the capacity to formulate their own questions. For a dozen strategies to enhance student questioning abilities, consider the online article, "Filling The Tool Box: Classroom Strategies to Engender Student Questioning." (Davis & McKenzie, 1984) http://fno.org/toolbox.html

Writing as Process

We are also beginning to see more and more clearly the interplay between writing, thinking and reading. To optimize the technology return on investment, we need to invest in substantial professional development designed to make sure all teachers know how to provide the kinds of support needed to make writing as process a fundamental program element.

Writing as process is essential if we want to see growth in student abilities because the model provides a basis for strategic intervention by teachers.

It turns out that the critical variable when improving student writing is prolonged, intimate and highly strategic teaching. The work of writing instructors such as Lucy Calkins, Peter Elbow and Linda Flower eloquently illustrates the extended journey required to achieve growth.

Writing improves when the writer internalizes an inventive process of reworking early efforts. Young people learn to be reflective and questioning about their own performance and efforts. They are both strategic and playful. They are versatile and fluent.

They develop a rich palette. They fill their toolkit with writing skills. They generate a "bag of tricks." They learn to shed the lazy, the cheap and the plastic in favor of the authentic and the genuine. They develop a passion for editing and revision.

Great writing teachers may prove an inspiration.

How? Dialogue. Extended engagement. Commitment. The process is commonly torturous and time-consuming. Teacher and student enjoy a highly personalized exchange that cannot be reduced to simple formulas or recipes. The process cannot be easily packaged or replicated. There is no compact twelve step program. It is an intensive human communion requiring persistence and devotion. Teacher and student consider intriguing issues like these:

- How can we capture meaning so that it still shines for others?
- How can we weave and organize our thoughts so they flow with just the right amount of dramatic tension?
- How might we extend our grasp of words and their meanings so as to avoid ho-hum, cookie-cutter sentences?
- How do I find my voice?

Acing the Standards

Effective writing teachers show their students how to extend their own growth, sharing models like the **Six Traits of Effective Writing** - an approach to revision. (Ruth Culham and Vicki Spandel)

http://www.nwrel.org/eval/pdfs/6plus1traits.pdf

They then encourage them to develop their own questions.

Questions to Ask about the Six Traits

Ideas and Content

How can I:

- Change the way I write my sentences so that the main ideas stand out more clearly?
- Add evidence or examples so that my ideas stand with enough support?
- Add details, testimony or information that will make my paper more convincing?
- Explain my reasons for not agreeing with opposing ideas and possibilities?
- Improve the logic of my argument?
- Strengthen the connections between ideas, examples and illustrations?

Questions for the remaining traits can be found online at http://fno.org//sept98/infolit5.html

Organization   **Voice**
Word Choice   **Sentence Fluency**
Conventions

2. Make Strategic Teaching a Priority

The secret to changing student performance is timely intervention by a skillful teacher who is constantly watching and diagnosing student efforts. As outlined in the next chapter, a teacher may intervene in four basic ways:

Acing the Standards

1. Adds to the student toolkit
2. Untangles wrong thinking
3. Empowers independent problem-solving
4. Encourages invention

The ability of the teacher to carry out this approach is directly related to her or his skill in questioning, without which the teacher will have difficulty diagnosing student patterns and routines. Questioning is at the heart of strategy.

"What can I do now?"
"What's going wrong?"
"What are my choices?"
"What has worked in the past?"

3. Identify & Practice the Sixty Toughest Questions

Regardless of the state, the same challenging questions and reading tasks occur over and over again.

- Can you suggest a better title for this passage?
- What was the author's purpose?
- What is the main point here?
- Can you tell what attitude the author might have toward (insert issue or subject) from this passage?
- What is wrong with the logic used by the author?
- What were the most important factors leading to the character's decision?

Schools need to make lists of such questions and then blend them into the daily lives of students so they encounter and practice them in social studies, math, science, art and all of the subject areas.

It is not enough to provide practice. Students must participate in group sessions during which a teacher may model an approach to that kind of question. We need to "surface" the inquiry process that works best for each of these questions rather than just assuming that all of our students may figure out the best strategy independently.

4. Emphasize Mindware

Some software programs can actually enhance the way we do our thinking. **Inspiration**, as mentioned above, is a kind of mindware that encourages a more visual approach to thinking. Sustained practice under the right conditions might help students to "put their heads around" some complex thinking processes.

In much the same way, various software tools such as spreadsheets can help students to do a different kind of data analysis and scenario testing - seeing what happens if variables change. This is precisely the kind of mathematical reasoning and inference required more and more often by state mathematics standards and tests.

Unfortunately, there is little evidence that these more "constructivist" uses of computer software have taken hold in classrooms.

Conclusion

In some respects the Internet and networked computers are only half a product - like a car without a highway, gas or destination, like a CD player without music, like a guitar without strings or strummer.

In all too many cases we have "put the cart before the horse."

Enamored with the glamor of networking and inspired by the workplace readiness arguments of futurists, we have rushed to place cables and computers in all classrooms without completing the design of the product.

What we have slighted in this process is the development of worthwhile learning experiences that would take advantage of the new technologies to achieve new levels of student performance. We have operated on the (mistaken) notion that equipment and access would translate into performance benefits.

The most important thing to remember is that great teaching is more important than great equipment!

Chapter 7 - Strategic Teaching

Strategic teaching requires thoughtful choices. An effective teacher has a toolkit of strategies that can dramatically modify student performance when the choice of tool fits the situation and the individual student. The best teachers are great at "sizing up" a student's patterns in order to figure out how to jump start improvement.

Intervention for Growth

Timely intervention is required in order to boost performance. Left undisturbed, most students routinely apply what they already know to tasks. But it is these routines - like flat tires - that often need changing.

Wrong routines lead to wrong answers.

Answering comprehension questions, the student may apply the following routine to the task:

"The main idea is always found in the first sentence."

The effective teacher steps in at the right time - intervenes - to bring about a burst of newly directed activity. The new direction radically improves performance.

In a society that opens and closes doors based upon test performance, strategic teaching creates more opportunities and richer choices. It confounds predictions based upon background. It supports upward mobility and provokes the blooming of talent. Strategic teaching frees potential from the grip of tradition, low expectations and apathy.

Strategic Teaching

Four Types of Intervention

Not all teacher interventions are appropriate, helpful or timely. There are four interventions that hold considerable promise, however, especially when they are applied in a customized fashion as a combination to match the student's profile.

1. Adds to the student toolkit as needed

As students pass through life and school, adults often hand them tools and show them new ways of doing things. Unfortunately, the timing of these adult gifts may not coincide with student need or readiness. Rather than grasping the gift and putting it to good use, the student may drop it on the way out the classroom door or may ignore its presence entirely. Later when the mental saw or drill might be most helpful, the student stands helpless and ill-prepared.

"What am I supposed to do with this mess?" they complain.

Just as rain may fall so heavily in a single hour that the ground cannot absorb it fast enough to prevent flooding and runoff, schools may bombard students with skills before they are ready to absorb and apply them.

One antidote to "skill runoff" is the teaching of skills in the context of real problems so that students see their value. But strategic teachers take this responsibility a step further. In addition to ongoing efforts to expand student toolkits in a developmental manner, they frequently monitor the toolkit of each student to see which tools have "slipped through the cracks." They intervene to provide each individual student with enough support to make essential tools a permanent part of the toolkit. They time intervention and support to match the challenges at hand.

2. Untangles wrong thinking

When students fail to perform, select wrong answers and end up in the wrong place at the wrong time, their difficulties may often be traced to tangled thinking and wrong rules. They approach the problem or challenge with the wrong operating procedures and the wrong strategies. Given more practice on the same kinds of problems, they are apt to keep right on with the tangled thinking and the wrong rules.

Effective teachers ask students to reveal the patterns of their thinking. "How did you come up with that answer?" they ask.

This diagnostic process is central to the intervention process. If teachers do not take the time to ask, it is unlikely that they will be able to match interventions to individual students. Remedial programs become parking lots instead of repair shops.

Once the teacher knows how the student is approaching the problem, the teacher may help to untangle the thinking and may suggest some better strategies to apply in the future.

3. Empowers independent problem-solving

The effective teacher rarely picks up the student's problem and rarely touches the student's mouse or track pad. The emphasis is firmly placed on developing independence and autonomy.

Noting that a pair of students seem stuck on their research path, spinning wheels without going any place, the teacher stands close by, listens in to the conversation and actually abstains from intervention until 15-20 minutes later, knowing that some frustration is basic to the creative process.

He knows that he must not jump in too quickly, thereby robbing the student team of authentic learning. He is aware that synthesis often requires some incubation and struggle. Content that the students are wrestling with the challenge in an earnest manner, he moves along to monitor the progress of other groups.

"Mr. Frederico? How can I get some decent information on crime?"

A student is tugging at his elbow insistently. He could simply tell the student to visit the Bureau of Justice. He could supply the URL. He could share some statistics already downloaded. But he wants this student to gain independence.

"Remember the strategy we discussed, **Going to the Source?** How do you think that might help here"

The student frowns at first, a bit irritated that the request has been turned back around. "You mean, like, figure out where it might be? Who might have the information?"

Mr. Frederico nods. "Sure. Who do you think has the best information on crime?"

The student's frown deepens. "The cops?"

Mr. Frederico smiles. "Keep going," he says. "In fact, I'd like you to go back to your laptop and make a list of six possible sources and then test them out on the Net. See which one proves most helpful."

4. Encourages invention of new tools & skills

Independent problem-solving often requires the invention of new tools and strategies. Sometimes it simply requires new ways of using old tools. One way or another, students must learn to modify their toolkit, making new tools and bending the old ones to the new tasks at hand.

"This isn't fair! They haven't taught me how to do that."

In times of rapid change, the unexpected is expected, the unthinkable is common, and the anomaly is commonplace. Students will need a "change ethic" in order to manage the inconsistencies and surprises that are so typical of life and learning in the Age of Information.

A change ethic involves a spirit of welcoming change and surprise along with a toolkit of strategies to manage those surprises. Effective teachers work on developing both the spirit and the toolkit, showing students how inventiveness pays off.

Networked schools must place a premium on students inventing new ways of doing things because so many encounters with technology involve learning new rules, new procedures and new operating procedures. Because many sites are "interactive," the visitor actually invents the visit by combining various features and exercising certain options.

Part Two

The Research Cycle

Chapter 8 - The Research Cycle

As the information landscape shifts to offer far more information in an often befuddling manner that some have called "data smog," many schools are learning that traditional approaches to student research are inadequate to meet the essential learning goals set by most states or provincial governments. With hundreds of computers and dozens of classrooms connected to extensive electronic information resources, schools are recognizing the importance of reinventing the way they engage students in both questioning and research.

In order to support broad-based adoption of effective questioning and research strategies, a district team comprised of teachers, teacher librarians and administrators should conduct a search for an effective research model. This team may compare and contrast the features and traits of a half dozen models in order to settle upon one that matches district needs and preferences. In some cases, they may build their own model, synthesizing the best features of each model reviewed.

Once the district has identified a model that seems compatible and compelling, all teachers are provided substantial professional development support to learn the model's features as they relate to their own subject assignments. Such professional development should include substantial opportunities for the adult learners to employ the research model to explore an essential adult question drawn from their own life or their subject area. To develop a comfortable level of competence with such a model (given most teachers' limited prior experience with this kind of research) usually requires 12-30 hours of professional development time. This may be 2-5 days of summer workshop time.

A Choice of Models

There are several excellent reviews currently available for those who wish to begin such a search. One is by David Loertscher, **A Taxonomy of Research Models**. Another summary and analysis is a chapter by Helen Thompson and Susan Henley, **Chapter 4 "Essential Components of Information Literacy: THE RESEARCH PROCESS,"** that reviews the following models:

♦ *The Big6 Skills Information Problem-Solving Approach to Information Skills Instruction,*™- Michael B. Eisenberg and Robert E. Berkowitz

♦ *INFOZONE*, from the Assiniboine South School Division of Winnipeg, Canada

♦ *Pathways to Knowledge*, Follett's Information Skills Model, by Marjorie Pappas and Ann Tepe

♦ *The Organized Investigator* (Circular Model) - David Loertscher and presented on the California Technology Assistance Project, Region VII's web site

♦ *The Research Cycle*, created - Jamie McKenzie

♦ *Information Literacy: Dan's Generic Model* - Dan Barron.

The purpose of this chapter is to present the **Research Cycle** in a concise and user friendly manner. Because such good work has already been done by those comparing and contrasting the other models, I will not duplicate their efforts here, other than to mention a special affinity with two of the models: *INFOZONE* and *The Organized Investigator* (Circular Model) because they offer much of the same emphasis upon questioning, exploration, synthesis and wondering that is intended by the **Research Cycle**.

Questioning First and Foremost

As will be shown in far more detail in subsequent chapters, when students explore truly demanding questions, they rarely know what they don't know when they first plan their investigations. They also tend to jump right into gathering without carefully mapping out the many questions they should be examining in their search for knowledge and understanding.

The **Research Cycle** differs from some models in its very strong focus upon essential questions and subsidiary questions early in the process. It also rejects topical research as being little more than information gathering unworthy of a student's time. Some other models are too easily converted into simple shopping trips. Students set out with a basket and enjoy an information binge, scooping up everything they can find about a state, a province, a foreign country, a famous person, a battle, a scientific issue or some item already conveniently available in containerized forms within some encyclopedia or book devoted to the subject. This kind of school research puts students in the role of **information consumers** and demands little thought, imagination or skill.

The **Research Cycle** puts students in the role of **information producers.** Like the two models mentioned earlier, *INFOZONE* and *The Organized Investigator* (Circular Model), **The Research Cycle** requires that students make up their own minds, create their own answers and show independence and judgment. Because students are actively revising and rethinking their research questions and plans throughout the process, they are forced to **cycle** back repeatedly through the stages listed below so that the more skill they develop, the less linear the process.

We teach teams of students to move repeatedly through each of the steps of the **Research Cycle** below:

The Research Cycle

QUESTIONING
PLANNING
GATHERING
SORTING & SIFTING
SYNTHESIZING
EVALUATING

——> REPORTING*

(Reporting comes after several repetitions of the cycle create sufficient INSIGHT)*

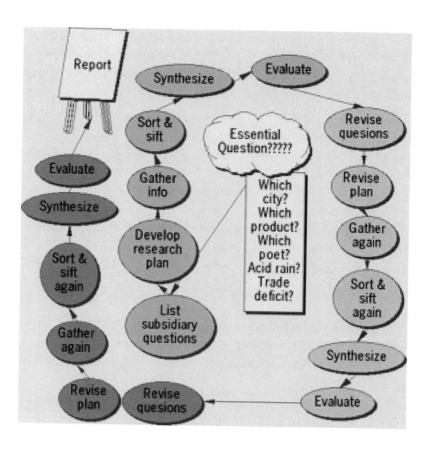

Cluster diagrams created with **Inspiration**™

The Research Cycle

Questioning

Unfortunately, much school research has been topical. Students were asked to "go find out about" Hitler or Connecticut or Adelaide. These assignments turned students into simple "word movers."

New technologies make word moving - "cutting and pasting" - quite ridiculous. We should now emphasize research questions that require problem-solving or decision-making, questions that cause students to make up their own minds and fashion their own answers.

"How might we restore the salmon harvest?"

"In which Asian city should our family spend a 2 year visit?"

The first step in the **Cycle** is to clarify and "map out" the dimensions of the essential question being explored. The student or student team begins by brainstorming to form a cluster diagram of all related questions. These subsidiary questions will then guide subsequent research efforts.

A class of second graders working with a teacher might create the following list of questions on **Inspiration™**, for example:

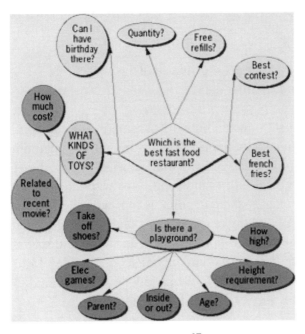

The Research Cycle

Planning

Finding Pertinent and Reliable information
After the student team has mapped out the research to be conducted, the next step is to think strategically about the best ways to find pertinent and reliable information that will help them to construct answers to these subsidiary questions.

Students consider now where the best information might lie?

"Is it readily available in a book?"

"Can I find it on a CD-ROM?"

"Would it be available on one of our district's networked periodical collections like SIRS or Electric Library?"

"If I go to the Internet, where should I start? a search engine like Altavista? a directory like Yahoo? the source site itself like the Census or the Federal Bureau of Justice?"

Which of these sources are most likely to provide reliable information with the most efficiency?

Wise students ask for help with this stage, turning to the school or public librarian.

"Where is the best source for crime statistics?"

"Where can I find weather data?"

While the first rush to install networks seemed to circumvent the library and the librarian in some places, many people are beginning to recognize the continuing value of **information mediation** - the guidance provided by a skillful information specialist who knows where the best information resides and can point us to it with the least fuss, bother and wasted time. Many teachers, for example, have come to rely on the Web suggestions of librarian (now technology director) Kathy Schrock at http://discoveryschool.com/schrockguide/ Instead of wading through hundreds of sites to find a few good social studies or math sites, they trust Kathy to do that for them.

The Research Cycle

Even though students once rushed around and past the librarian on the way to the computer and the Internet, a few hundred hours of fruitless searching often seems to reduce student enthusiasm for random prospecting and surfing. Eager to get on with their project or inquiry, they turn to more reliable and well organized sources and they begin to welcome the "pointers" offered by a good librarian.

Thinking About Selection, Storage and Retrieval

In a time of information abundance (some would say "infoglut"), it is folly to jump into gathering without first giving careful thought to strategies for targeting and then storing the most relevant information. This early planning will greatly reduce the need for sorting and sifting later on. It will also contribute to the building of new ideas by empha-sizing what information specialists call "signal" (information that illuminates) over "noise" (information that befuddles).

Studying a city like San Francisco in order to compare it with San Diego and LA and make a choice, they might find more than 2 million Web pages ("hits") using a search engine like Altavista.

Their first findings? A Chevy dealer, a hair stylist, a whole bunch of e-mail messages and a bunch of files that might cast little light on their search.

But they want to know if this city meets their criteria! Is it safe?

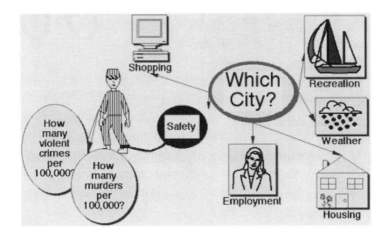

The Research Cycle

In many cases, students confuse "hits" on a search engine with progress toward insight and understanding. Since there was some tendency to reward length in times past and to confuse the quantity of information with the quality of the research, students may watch their accumulating mountain of "hits" with glee, not appreciating that they have been constructing the equivalent of an information landfill with any treasures concealed from view.

It doesn't help to gather 600 files about crime in San Francisco. What the student must do is ask **telling questions** such as "What is the homicide rate per hundred thousand and how has it been changing during the past decade?"

If they are asking telling questions, then they are only keeping the most important findings, and they are storing them where they belong.

If they use their cluster diagram for note-taking, they simply attach their findings as notes to the relevant part of the diagram.

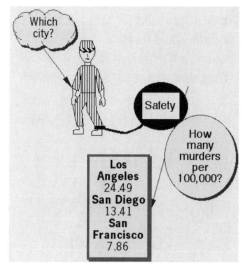

A more challenging way to accomplish the same thing electronically is to set up a database file like the one outlined and explained in Chapter Thirteen. Once students have collected several hundred entries, they will find this system very helpful for sorting their findings by key concepts.

The Research Cycle

Source: (Author, Title, Date, URL)
Subject:
Keywords:
Abstract:

The goal of this step of planning for research is to create a storage system that will protect students from accumulating huge mountains of information in hundreds of poorly named files. Retrieval from such a "hodge podge" can be a daunting task.

We also hope to dissuade students from wholesale cutting and pasting. By planning ahead they will have an information storage system that will eventually support concept-based retrieval, synthesis, and analysis.

Organizing gathering around key ideas, categories and questions increases the likelihood that gathering will induce, provoke and inspire thought. Under older models, students gathered first and tended to think (if at all) later. We hope to maintain the tension of good questions, the cognitive dissonance and energy explored in Chapter Four - "Students in Resonance."

Gathering

If the planning has been thoughtful and productive, the team proceeds to satisfying information sites swiftly and efficiently, gathering only that information that is relevant and useful. Otherwise, teams might wander for many hours, scooping up hundreds of files that will later prove frustrating and valueless.

It is critically important that findings are structured **as they are**

gathered. Putting this task off until later is very dangerous when coping with **infoglut**. It is also crucial that students only use the Internet when likely to provide the best information. In many cases, books, CD-ROMs and other networked information will prove more efficient and more useful.

Sorting and Sifting

The more complex the research question, the more important the sorting and sifting providing the data supporting the next stage - **synthesis**. Much selecting and sorting should occur place during the previous stage - **gathering** - but now the team moves toward even more systematic scanning and organizing of data to set aside and organize those nuggets most likely to contribute to **insight**. The team sorts and sifts the information much as a fishing boat must cull the harvest brought to the surface in a net.

Synthesizing

In a process akin to jigsaw puzzling, the students arrange and rearrange the information fragments until patterns and some kind of picture begin to emerge. Synthesis is fueled by the tension of a powerful research question. This stage is fully outlined in Chapter Four - "Students in Resonance" and again in Chapter Fourteen - "Regrouping Findings."

Evaluating

At this point, the team asks if more research is needed before proceeding to the **reporting** stage. In the case of complex and demanding research questions, students must usually complete several repetitions of the **Cycle** since they usually do not know what they don't know when they first plan their research. The timing of the reporting and sharing of insights is determined by the quality of the "information harvest" during this EVALUATION stage.

Reporting

As multimedia presentation software becomes readily available to our schools and our students, we are seeing movement toward persuasive presentations. The research team, charged with making a decision or creating a solution, reports its findings and its recommendations to an audience of decision-makers (simulated or real). Chapter Fifteen describes this process in considerable detail while warning against the glib and superficial, flashy multimedia reports that are becoming fashionable in all too many places.

Chapter 9 - Planning the Voyage

Introduction: The Surf is Down

While it was fashionable in the early days of the Internet - even in educational circles - to speak of "surfing" the Net in reverential terms and tones, as if time browsing the Net were a sufficient end in itself, mere surfing can be as productive as hours spent in some arcade bombing aliens. The Internet is a vast hodgepodge of information resources thrown together with very little planning, structure or quality control. Wandering aimlessly across the Net's shimmering surface or delving haphazardly through its labyrinthine menus may be addictive, but students can easily squander hours without gaining any new insight or valuable information.

In 2000, few educators brag to parents that students may "surf" the Net.

Library media specialists and teachers face a new instructional challenge: showing a generation of students how to plan and conduct meaningful research with the prodigious electronic information resources now becoming as widely available as ATMs. While most staff development for the Internet has hitherto focused upon how to gain access and drive the electronic highway, we should begin to focus on how to plan and execute thoughtful inquiry before, during and after our drives.

The next six chapters trace the development of a student project stage by stage from beginning to end, emphasizing the information problem-solving skills needed for success with the Internet and other sources during each stage.

This chapter identifies the kinds of planning that should occur before the students even venture out onto the Net.

1. Creating a Research Team

Effective inquiry with vast resources suggests group research rather than solo flights. This is the model in the workplace. It should become a frequent school experience. Groups make sense when exploring vastness, and they also make sense when online time may be limited.

Readers can consult the vast literature on cooperative and collaborative learning to expand knowledge of how groups work well together on such tasks, but a few simple guidelines will save a good deal of time and trouble:

Teams of 3-4 students are formed with the skills of the members a paramount consideration. The teacher may wish to assign class members to groups in order to provide balance, insure harmony and increase the likelihood that the teams will function productively.

Each member might be assigned a particular role (navigator, helmsperson, recorder) and all should receive a clear outline of individual and group performance expectations.

For an example, teachers from Kulshan Middle School in Bellingham, Washington developed the following rubrics to clarify the group research process: http://bham.wednet.edu/online/volcano/daily.htm

Process:
    5
        • Participates actively
        • Models caring about goals
        • Helps direct the group in setting goals
        • Helps direct group in meeting goals
        • Thoroughly completes assigned tasks

Planning the Voyage

3
• Participates in group
• Shows concern for goals
• Participates in goal setting
• Participates in meeting goals
• Completes assigned tasks

1
• Chooses not to participate
• Shows no concern for goals
• Impedes goal setting process
• Impedes group from meeting goals
• Does not complete assigned task

The Oak Harbor Rubrics also outline research expectations. (http://fno.org/libskill.html)

Prior to actual research, teams should have one opportunity to see the functioning of a research team, either with an appropriate video-tape or through teacher modeling.

Assessment procedures should be clarified up front.

II. Framing Essential Questions

We are fighting a long school history of topical research. For decades students have been sent to the library to "find out about" some topic. This tradition has led to information gathering but little analysis or thought.

Essential questions set students and staff free from this tedious and wasteful ritual. Research becomes motivating and meaningful. An essential question has the following attributes:

Essential questions reside at the top of Bloom's Taxonomy (Bloom, 1954). They require students to EVALUATE (make a thoughtful choice between options, with the choice based upon clearly stated criteria), to SYNTHESIZE (invent a new or different version) or to ANALYZE (develop a thorough and complex understanding through skillful questioning).

Essential questions spark our curiosity and sense of wonder. They derive from some deep wish to understand some thing that matters to us.

Answers to essential questions cannot be found. They must be invented. It is something like cooking a great meal. The researcher goes out on a shopping expedition for the raw ingredients, but "the proof is in the pudding." Students must construct their own answers and make their own meaning from the information they have gathered. They create insight.

Answering such questions may take a life time, and even then, the answers may only be tentative ones. This kind of research, like good writing, should proceed over the course of several weeks, with much of the information gathering taking place outside of formally scheduled class hours.

Essential questions engage students in the kinds of real life applied problem-solving suggested by nearly every new curriculum report.

Essential questions usually lend themselves well to multidisciplinary investigations, requiring that students apply the skills and perspectives of math and language arts while wrestling with content from social studies or science.

It would be best if students could learn to frame their own Essential questions, but in most cases they will require several experiences with teacher generated questions before they can shed years of practice with trivial information-gathering questions.

Here are three middle school examples:

EVALUATION

"With the economy shifting and changing, families are sometimes forced to move to entirely different regions in order to find jobs. Imagine that the families in your team are all moving from the West Coast to New England. Create a multimedia presentation that you might share with your parents recommending the best New England city to move to from the following list of cities. Your choice must be based upon the availability of jobs your parents can fill and other criteria identified and listed by your team related to categories such as recreation, education, entertainment, climate, etc. You must compare and contrast three cities."

SYNTHESIS

"There is much disagreement among people who plan for student use of the Internet regarding what kinds of access should be permitted. Some people are afraid that students will come into contact with offensive materials. Others are afraid that limitations will limit student's freedoms. Imagine that your team has been assigned the task of revising the attached sample policy from School District X. Compare this policy with others from around the nation and then produce a list of recommended amendments, explaining your reasons for each of your suggestions. You will prepare a persuasive multimedia presentation as if speaking before the district's board of education."

ANALYSIS

"Some people think that CD-ROM "edutainment products" may do damage to young people. What seem to be the biggest risks people see connected with such products and what evidence can you find to dispute or substantiate their fears? Create a persuasive multimedia report that might appear on the evening news as a consumer advisory for parents."

When teams are engaged in responding to questions that require this kind of thinking, there is little danger that they will be satisfied with "surfing" the Net. After an hour of surfing they are likely to start complaining. "This isn't getting us anywhere!"

Planning the Voyage

III. Identifying Subsidiary questions

One of the first steps students take in their teams is the listing of smaller questions that will help them answer their main question. They need to understand how large questions are really the parent and grandparent of many related questions, all of which can nest within the largest question like small Russian dolls. Effective research results from formulating as many categories of related questions as possible, with each category suggesting missing questions.

When a team begins the task of selecting a city in New England, for example, they must list selection criteria related to categories such as climate. "What do we want to know about climate?" the team asks. "I don't like cold weather!" complains one member. "OK, then, what are the highs and lows and average temperatures for each city. What else do we want to know?"

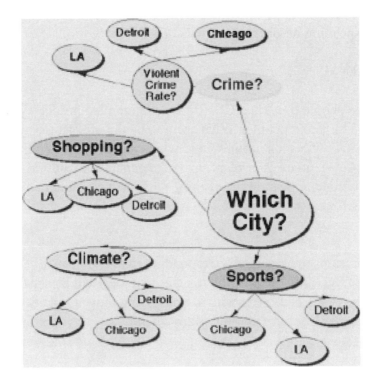

Planning the Voyage

The most powerful subsidiary questions are "Telling questions." These are very carefully phrased so they go right to the heart of the matter like "smart bombs." They eliminate wandering around and aimless gathering.

Want to know which city is safest?

"What is the rate of violent crime as reported by the FBI for each of our cities and how has it changed in the past 10 years?"

IV. Stating Suppositions - Hypothesizing and Predicting

Before they proceed very far, students list suppositions, pose hypotheses and make predictions - many and most of which will be revised as information is gathered. This thought process helps to provide a basis for construction of meaning.

Marty and Jacqueline Brooks' 1993 ASCD publication **In Search of Understanding: the Case for Constructivist Classrooms** makes a great primer describing this student thought process.

The Brooks stress the importance of students stating suppositions early in the planning process. The research team is speculating. "What do you suppose? Why do you suppose? How do you suppose?" Heeding their intuition and checking their previous experience or knowledge base, students list their best guesses, their hunches, their conjectures. These are shots in the dark. Research then brings light to the subject. Information proves illuminating. Students revise their guesswork. They reconstruct meaning.

V. Browsing Resources to Identify Worthwhile Sources

Because the Internet is a monstrously disorganized mishmash of resources with very little quality control or reliable searching mechanisms, it is possible to waste whole days wandering around in information purgatory. Not only is much of the information unreliable, it is also difficult to find. Many of the words associated in Roget's Thesaurus (1987) with "mishmash" are perfectly apt:

> confusion, welter, jumble, shambles, mix-up, medley,
> embroilment, imbroglio, wilderness, jungle, chaos, muddle,
> litter, clutter, mess, mishmash, hash, hodgepodge, ragbag,
> witch's brew, jumble, grab bag, Babel, bedlam, madhouse

Students must learn quite early that it pays to identify reliable resources before logging onto the Internet, using one of the many very useful hard copy guides. These guides help to point students toward good information along paths that minimize wasted menu searching.

Students must also consider the value of competing resources such as print materials and networked resources of various kinds that might offer more organization, more reliability and less noise. To optimize results, they will "look before they leap" and devote time to those resources most likely to cast light on their research questions.

VII. Developing Research Strategies

Once a student research team has passed through the steps outlined above, they begin matching resources to questions and they begin thinking about how they will collect their findings as they proceed. Unfortunately, it is seductively easy to gather dozens of files and hundreds of pages of text while visiting the Net. If these are not properly sorted and stored from the very beginning, with at least some level of culling taking place as the search proceeds, the sorting and sifting process to be described in later articles will prove nightmarish.

A student research plan will resemble a cluster diagram with all of the subsidiary questions flowing out of the essential question and a list of sources associated with each question.

Once they venture onto the Net, students may store findings in files structured to match the questions or in a database with codes and keywords to match those questions and categories.

Planning the Voyage

Conclusion

The value of student time spent on the Internet will increase ten fold if a great deal of time is devoted to planning the journey into Cyberspace instead of grabbing an electronic surfboard and rushing to the beach unprepared. The vastness of the resources are both a curse and a blessing, for students are ill-prepared by the past traditions of school research (which emphasized information-gathering within narrow boundaries) to handle the Internet's "wide open spaces."

School media specialists and teachers who provide students with a strong foundation in questioning and planning will soon see the dividends when students return from journeys flushed with success. "Look, Mrs. Vance. You won't believe what we discovered!"

In many cases, students will report that the best information emerged from source other than the Internet.

Chapter 10 - The Hunt

Introduction: After the Planning - The Hunt

The preceding chapter stressed the importance of framing research projects around Essential Questions instead of topics, and it outlined ways to optimize students' effectiveness by planning before they actually venture onto the Net or start gathering information from other sources. This chapter and the next will emphasize "Great Hunting" as a theme, highlighting research skills and practices likely to contribute to the development of insight.

1. Hunting with an Open Mind

What is an open mind?

A mind that welcomes new ideas. A mind that invites new ideas in for a visit. A mind that introduces new ideas to the company that has already arrived. A mind that is most comfortable in mixed company. A mind that prizes silence and reflection. A mind that recognizes that later is often better than sooner.

An open mind is not the same as an empty mind. An open mind is one leaning toward meaning, hungry for connections, avidly seeking patterns and insight. An open mind is filled with great questions - questions spawned by curiosity, questions planned by the research team, questions that keep giving birth to new ones as the research proceeds and the puzzle develops. The old research was content with filling an empty mind. "Go find out about!"

Researching used to be mere gathering. Hunting, on the other hand, suggests a more thoughtful and more aggressive approach - one imbued with the tension arising from the building of meaning out of scattered pieces and what seems all too often like nonsense.

This is no mere collecting. It is collection with a purpose. The bits and pieces, the raw data, the summaries and the clues one chooses to keep are all meant to help solve the jigsaw puzzle presented by the team's essential question.

Take the middle school project that asks a team to select a New England city to that their families might move. The old way of studying a state or city required mere listings of products, weather conditions or other attributes. The new research requires sifting through employment data to assess how healthy various job sectors might be over the next decade. It's not enough to find that there are jobs in your parents' skill areas. The team must evaluate whether there are openings and whether or not the need for those jobs will grow or decline. Even then the work is not done. How does this city compare with the other two cities under investigation?

It is no longer sufficient to list the art museums or the parks or the sports teams. One must assess the quality of each as it relates to the family values and preferences. What good is a museum with a weak collection of dowdy landscapes? What good is a park too dangerous to enter in broad daylight? What good is a sports team that never scores?

An open mind is essential because it provides the spirit, the momentum, and the drive for the research team to push through the Infoglut so often typical of the Internet. An open-minded researcher learns to "peer inward" to see what is missing, what is unknown, what needs discovering.

The old research was **additive**. The student did not need to reexamine what she or he knew or was learning. There was no need to challenge old thinking or preconceptions. The student cast a net for facts. The new research is **generative**.

One student interviewed me for 30 minutes before cutting off the discussion and thanking me.

"Thanks, Dr. McKenzie, but I cannot use anything you shared with me today."

The Hunt

"Why is that?" I asked, disappointed and surprised.

"Everything you told me undermines my thesis statement, that we will not need books and libraries when we have the Internet."

"But can't you change your thesis statement based on new knowledge and discoveries?"

"No," she answered, "we are marked down if we change our thesis statement."

The antithesis of research!

The search for insight requires continual reexamination of old beliefs, prior knowledge and stored information in order to reconstruct, rearrange and synthesize the elements into new meanings.

Students rarely appear on the classroom doorstep with open minds. While they may have encountered some classes where this kind of thinking is encouraged, the basic culture of schools created by the test-makers and the textbook makers has been dedicated to memorization rather than the making of meaning. If a teacher values student thinking, it will often be necessary to spend some time exploring the difference between an empty and an open mind.

II. Employing Effective Search Strategies

Many electronic information products provide keyword searching capabilities, but few schools have instituted effective student learning experiences that would help them become skillful searchers. Without such skills, Infoglut will present a serious challenge.

We are told that we can rely upon artificial intelligence to do the searching for us, that "natural language searching" will save us from the tedium of building logical searches, but the effectiveness of searching is enhanced dramatically by learning the "tricks of the trade."

Students need to learn all of the following in order to perform efficient and effective searches. Many can be practiced on CD-ROM encyclopedias or with collections of articles.

The Hunt

1. LOGICAL OPERATORS

Each search engine may use variations of the following logical operators (AND, OR, NOT, NEAR). It pays to read the HELP menu before using a search engine.

Logical operators allow the searcher to look for the intersection of "sets" of articles. The logic behind this kind of searching is called Boolean Logic - based on algebraic set theory.

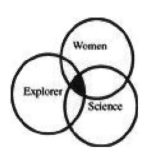

In the example on the left, the researcher is looking for articles or Web pages that contain all three of the words, "Women" AND "Explorer" AND "Science." Each circle represents the set of all Web pages containing a particular word. The intersection of the three circles shows the Web pages that contain all three.

Logical operators can direct and narrow a search toward useful sources. They can help us carve into the mountain of information to find the most pertinent and valuable material.

AND - When placed between two words (salmon AND fisheries) the program searches for documents that contain BOTH words anywhere in the document.

OR - When placed between two words (salmon OR fisheries) the program searches for documents that contain either of those words. This will usually return too large a sample unless the OR search is combined with an AND search, with the first word being fairly broad and the OR being used with a series of related words that are within parentheses -. "salmon AND (conservation OR extinct OR preservation)" This operator has the often unfortunate tendency to throw too big a net and is generally discouraged, but there are some wonderful times to use it.

NOT - This operator helps to eliminate unwanted articles. When placed between two words (salmon NOT Atlantic) the program searches for articles that contain the first but not the second word.

NEAR - When placed between two words (salmon NEAR fisheries) the program searches for documents that contain those words within a certain word range of each other. Many programs are set by default at 50 words but can usually be reset by the searcher. If students play with various settings, they may see vastly different search results. Just because two words appear in the same article does not mean they are related to each other meaningfully. If they are within 10 words, the odds improve that they are related.

2. TRUNCATION

comput*

Students learn to search for the base of a word and any of its variations. Each program may have a different symbol. Some use a question mark (?) and others use an asterisk (*).

computer	computerize	computerdom
computerist	computerese	computerized
compute	computing	

3. WILD CARDS

Some programs allow the searcher to insert a symbol inside a word that can stand for any letter(s). "Bl?nd" finds words like the following in my electronic dictionary:

bland	blend	blind
blond	blent	moonblind
purblind		

4. THESAURUS

Because most students do not have sufficient vocabularies to call up the words that might produce the best "hits," we might show them how to generate good lists with the thesaurus that now accompanies most good word processing programs. Looking for articles that cover strategies to protect the salmon harvest?

"Conservation," the thesaurus tells us, might be replaced by related words such as:

preservation	protection	saving
deliverance	conservationism	conservancy
ecology	management	perpetuation
prolongation	preserve	sanctuary
refuge	protected species	

5. INTUITIVE PLAY

Successful searching is a trial-and-error process of trying out various word combinations until the searcher hits "pay dirt." Sometimes the most logical word searches turn up nothing worth reading. If early efforts turn up just a handful of articles, it often pays to skim those articles looking for unusual words that the searcher might never have thought of using. "Fisheries" is a word I discovered in this manner - a word outside my normal usage that led to many other (often Canadian) articles about salmon conservation efforts.

Students will have the most success if they allow themselves the freedom of many trials, many attempts and many guesses.

III. Navigating in the Dark

Essential questions almost always require students to explore the unknown - darkness. They will spend their time striving for illumination. They will "cast light" upon their subject.

It is no accident that many boat chartering companies refuse to allow their customers to navigate in the dark. Darkness shifts perception and creates confusing illusions.

Accustomed to the old kind of research that required little navigating, little searching and little uncertainty, many students may find the process frustrating and irritating. They may demand the informational equivalent of fast food.

"Could you just tell us where to look!"

"Just what are we looking for?"

The print encyclopedia was the Big Mac of school research.

Too much school research has focused on moving around what we already know. This required little student thought.

School research has too often been like the man searching for his lost car keys under a street lamp. When a passerby asks if he lost his keys nearby, the man says, "No. But I'm looking here because the light is good."

Because this new kind of research can be frustrating and difficult at times, teachers might prepare students for the emotional aspects by appealing to their sense of adventure and exploration, drawing parallels with the great inventors and explorers of human history. They might also draw connections with the work of detectives.

IV. Navigating in the Mud

The New Information Landscape offers information mud flats - vast expanses of soft data and opinion that can bog us down and slow our search for truth. Students must learn to skirt the shoals unless they are seeking shellfish buried within. Just as students can bog down on certain test items and miserably fail a test, they can spend too long with resources that have little to offer. The best way to navigate in the mud, of course, is to avoid it or get out of it swiftly. Reliance upon printed guides is one strategy. Another is to learn discernment - making wise choices based on titles and other indicators.

V. Identifying the Unknowns

As the research team begins to collect useful information, the puzzle represented by the original question should begin to take shape

-even though the shape may keep shifting with the addition of each new insight. Considering essential questions is a bit like peering into a kaleidoscope. As the research proceeds, it is as if someone is turning the tube and shifting the perspective.

The team should frequently revisit, review and revise the original research plan that contained the list of questions and information targets. As they begin to piece together fragments into meaningful combinations, what they have gathered will begin to give shape to what is missing. The appearance of certain categories, for example, will suggest missing members of those categories as well as entirely new missing categories. Just as the first assembled pieces of a jigsaw puzzle suggest the shape of those pieces that need to be added next, early research begins to suggest later research.

Conclusion

Hunting for good information in the new information landscape requires a great deal of skill as well as the willingness to heed intuition. Once the fad has passed and the Internet is as much a part of everyday life as TV advertising, the glamor will wear off and mere surfing will hold little appeal. The value of various sources for students will depend greatly upon the kinds of information problem-solving skills they possess and employ. Open minds equipped with navigational ability will fare much better than the untutored.

Chapter 11 - More Hunting

Extending the Hunt

The preceding two chapters illustrated how student teams may design research projects around essential questions, how they must plan in advance of gathering information, and how they should be acquiring data in a dynamic, generative fashion with an open mind intent upon developing insight and new knowledge. Research requires students to reexamine old beliefs, prior knowledge and stored information in order to reconstruct, rearrange and synthesize the elements into new meanings.

This chapter extends the theme of "hunting" beyond the keyword searching and navigating outlined in the previous chapter.

I. Learning on the run

The old kind of school research required little new thinking as the gathering proceeded. The main challenge was finding "the right stuff." There were certain facts - such as the primary raw materials available in Kenya - that one sought, captured (on index cards) and then added to one's collection. It was a bit like filling the cages of a zoo.

Because certain school research assignments have been repeated for decades, many of the information products (such as encyclopedias) aimed at the school market carefully structured their information to conform to such assignments. The typical state, province or country article in an encyclopedia is laid out in sections that match perfectly with the research categories I was assigned as a student in 1960. A decade later, as a young social studies teacher, I passed along the ritual. In schools I visit today, I can find the same exercise being repeated in countries around the globe. Sadly, certain school experiences seem universal.

More Hunting

Which came first, it seems fair to ask, the encyclopedia or the state report?

Now the challenge is changing dramatically as megabytes of information scroll past student researchers. One is reminded of grey wolf packs or Sioux braves on horseback hunting great herds of migrating bison or elk. Which of the thousands of beasts thundering past are worth attacking? What's the best strategy to finish the day feasting?

The student who is trying to compare the employment opportunities or colleges in three New England cities using the U.S. Census (http://www.census.gov) or the Excite Travel (http://www.excite.com/travel/countries/united_states/) resources on the World Wide Web will not find answers waiting in neatly wrapped packages ready for downloading and capture. Raw data and information, yes. Answers, no.

Learning on the run requires students to change their way of thinking as well as the content of their thinking itself as they are in the act of scanning and gathering the data.

Because each site organizes its information differently, students must learn strategies that will work for each site. In the case of the U.S. Census, for example, the software will require the information consumer to answer a series of questions in order to identify the geographical entity (County? City?) and the type of data desired.

Once the student gains access to the data, itself, the data will often appear in forms and formats that do little to support insight. The designer of the Excite pages for Cambridge may have compiled dozens of pages about dozens of colleges, but the data will prove overwhelming and so immense as to obscure insight. The student learns that there are many colleges, but how do they compare with the higher education opportunities in the other cities?

How does one even think about colleges? Is it better to have many colleges in a city or just one great one? How do you know if Harvard is better than Bennington? How much of the information on Excite is written by city promoters intent on luring tourist dollars, students and new citizens? Which information can be trusted?

Real research begins with considerable ignorance about the topic being studied. If the question is really challenging, chances are the research team had difficulty developing a research plan at the outset and will need to revisit and revise the plan as research proceeds.

Learning on the run is the process (and skill) of revising strategies, questions and resources while conducting the research. Growing insight shifts the researchers' views of how and what to explore.

II. Changing course

The journey will lead up blind canyons and sometimes prove frustrating. Effective exploration may require the energy and flexibility of a pin ball jumping and bouncing around at incredible speed. Because the Internet offers dozens of seemingly promising sites that all too often prove disappointing, students must learn to assess the value of sites right away without wasting time on extended visits. They must move on quickly to better sites if the information seems weak.

While Chapter Nine argued the value of advance planning and identification of good resources, there is no way to avoid low quality information in today's information world.

III. Exploiting serendipity

The American Heritage Dictionary defines serendipity as "The faculty of making fortunate discoveries by accident." If one is too linear, too sequential, too logical and too intent on supporting what one already knows, one overlooks the clues that might lead to surprising new perspectives. One must be "on the lookout" for surprise or it can slide right by unnoticed. It turns out that the discoveries are not accidental after all. They just seem surprising because they differ markedly from previous ways of thinking and seeing.

To the open-minded, the Internet offers surprise after surprise. The breadth and often illogical structure of its offerings are both a curse and a blessing. The disorganization can prove frustrating and inefficient, but the hodgepodge is often delightfully inspirational.

"I never would have dreamed. "

Especially for research aimed at inventing or discovering something new, serendipity can be a great boost to thinking.

Corporate trainers from groups like Synectics devote long hours teaching groups to develop novel solutions to problems with strategies that intentionally take people beyond their normal ways of thinking.

Those who wish to restore the salmon harvest may learn more from efforts to protect the East African rhino than by studying what has been done for (or to) salmon so far in the Northwest. In searching for articles including the word "extinction," the student picks up the rhino article "by accident."

The old model for school research ignores and discards the rhino article. The new model says, "Let's give it a try." Perhaps there's an idea or strategy in there that would work for salmon that we haven't tried.

Even though our culture often conspires to protect us from surprise, much of the power of the Internet is to help us escape the boxes within which we live. We have carefully screened out information most of our lives. We are too often the prisoners of our cultures, our educational experiences and our biases. The Internet may set us free or reinforce us narrow-minded thinking. The choice is ours.

Research aimed at solving problems (restoring the salmon harvest) or making thoughtful decisions (selecting a city) thrives on surprise, but schools have too long striven to eliminate surprise from the school day. An information society requires workers and citizens who can challenge the old mind-sets and paradigms, inventing new approaches to adapt to a turbulent and rapidly changing world.

IV. Asking for help

Help menus are meant to expand our capabilities and improve our efficiency before we get in trouble. Unfortunately, many people are reluctant to employ the help menus until they are hopelessly mired in problems.

More Hunting

The Internet is actually made up of many information centers, each of which may have its own software with its own peculiar or unique set of rules and procedures. Ranging through dozens of different information sources, the searcher often encounters conflicting and confusing command structures. To prevent gridlock and wasted time, it makes sense to browse the help menu of these sources early in the visit, figuring out just what is and is not possible. "You mean I could have saved that file? If only I had known!"

Even though HELP is prominently displayed on most search engine menus, many users never read through the instructions to discover the powerful features that can help reduce the mountain of "hits" and target the more valuable sites.

We need to encourage students to check out the help menu first thing upon arriving at a site. Exploring Internet sites without checking out the help menu is like driving a standard transmission car without learning to shift.

V. Asking for directions

Some people will drive around totally lost for an hour before they will stop to ask directions. This same approach on the Internet gives new meaning to the word "lost." The potential for wasted time "circling the block" is magnified a hundred fold.

It makes sense to have several Internet guides or a skilled librarian nearby to call upon when lost. Commentators claim that the Internet is often "arcane. "Many of the people who have organized the menus, the pages and the directories seem to have passed up any courses in logic. They often fail to organize the resources with any structure that would guide us toward information in a logical manner. Unclear labels and titles for files make matters worse.

One way to reduce the threat that the Internet will prove Sphinx-like or enigmatic is to explore with a friendly guide close to hand, whether that guide be printed or human. Because many students may be unaccustomed to reaching out for such assistance and the old competitive model did little to promote cooperation, teachers and library media specialists face quite a challenge teaching this generation to stop and ask before they are lost.

Conclusion

Skillful hunting, mining or fishing are more appropriate as metaphors for student research in this new information environment than the once popular reference to surfing. Surfing may capture the essence of recreational use of electronic sources, but it fails to encompass the array of strategies required for students to find good information upon which new insights may be grounded. Now that we have considered that array of strategies, it is time to move to a consideration of how students might begin to sort and sift the information they have gathered.

Chapter 12 - Needles from Haystacks

Now that we have looked at hunting, it is time to consider how students might begin to sort and sift the information they gather.

It has become so easy to find and collect data that students can save hundreds of pages in a matter of moments. Not so long ago, I downloaded the entire text of **Moby Dick**, by accident, in about five minutes while trying to copy a single page. We must guide students to understand that abundance and volume may have little connection with wisdom and insight. To achieve insight, students must learn to fashion needles from haystacks. It is less a matter of finding answers than the challenge of constructing them from bits and pieces, odds and ends.

Collecting and gathering is easy. Making meaning is far more difficult and yet far more worthwhile, especially at a time when state standards emphasize inferential reasoning, interpretation and synthesis.

1. Keeping track of findings

The wise researcher designs a way to collect the most meaningful fragments, information and ideas in an easily searchable, compact location. For decades we have been showing students how to accomplish this task with index cards, but the time has come to replace cards with cluster diagrams or database files that support the culling and organizing process. No more drilling holes through note cards! It is important to maintain notes in an electronic format to support the construction of new ideas because the information is more easily transformed (sorted, sifted, grouped and modified) while electronic.

Each time a student or team of students finds worthwhile information, the best parts should be saved while preserving the citation and a focus on the most valuable elements. As was discussed in Chapter

Needles from Haystacks

Eight, either a cluster diagram or database file can be effective in supporting this kind of information storage.

```
Source: (Author, Title, Date, URL)
Subject:
Keywords:
Abstract:
```

In the case of the students working as teams to compare and contrast three cities in New England, the database can be set up in advance with 75-100 records partially completed to help to guide the hunting outlined in the previous chapters as well as the sorting which occurs later.

The students paste the names of the five cities in the SUBJECT field until there are 20 records for each city. They then paste in several KEYWORDS for each city which match the selection criteria agreed upon by the team. If a team wanted a city . . .

With a low crime rate: Keyword=Crime
With good colleges: Keyword=College
With winning sports teams: Keyword=Sports
With safe and inviting parks: Keyword=Parks
With attractive shopping: Keyword=Shopping
With employment opportunity: Keyword=Jobs
With activities for teenagers: Keyword=Entertainment

While hunting, then, students take the records (just like index cards) for particular cities (all of Portland) or particular keywords (crime in all 3 cities) and hunt for information that will provide a basis for choice. Once they find good information, they may paste sentences, key ideas and valuable items into the ABSTRACT field, noting the source information (TITLE, AUTHOR, SOURCE, DATE, PAGE, etc.) in the other fields.

Needles from Haystacks

Note: Cutting and Pasting can be the enemy of thinking and reading! Make sure your students are selective in their collecting. Better to paraphrase than cut and paste.

A similar process may be used with a word processing file, but it will prove far less valuable when it comes time to analyze and synthesize the findings. It is far more difficult to sort, sift and search the findings.

II. Screening and compacting info-garbage

Because it is now quite easy to locate and download hundreds of pages of information, we must place a high priority on showing students how to save the "right stuff," discarding that which is irrelevant or unlikely to contribute to understanding.

The student who visits Boston or Cambridge sites hoping to learn about colleges, quickly finds a large list:

Boston University - Harvard - Institute of Politics at the Kennedy School of Government -Lesley College - MIT- School of The Museum of Fine Arts -Northeastern University -Tufts University - Wellesley College

The list can be pasted in the ABSTRACT of one Cambridge record. But so what? How much does this list really mean to a 13 year old? How much do they now know about the quality of these colleges and universities?

It will take much further reading, considering and evaluating to explore the quality question. A list says little in itself. With the World Wide Web, each item is a button. "Click" on Boston University and the student finds an overwhelming amount of information, much of it carefully crafted by skilled marketing folks who wish to make the campus appear safe and attractive. If they have problem with muggings or date rape, it is unlikely to appear on these pages.

There is no longer any shortage of fresh and pertinent data to review. The student has a much deeper basis for asking whether the city offers good educational opportunities.

Needles from Haystacks

As the research proceeds, the students cull the essential, meaningful and reliable data. The garbage is set aside, compacted and discarded. The student establishes criteria for reliability and applies them to separate wheat from chaff. Key action verbs: choose, pick, select, separate, sift, and single out.

As students explores new resources, they continually ask screening and compacting questions:

Screening and Compacting Questions

"Is this data worth keeping?"

"Will this information shed light on our question?"

"Is this information reliable?"

"How much of this information do I need to place in my database?"

"How can I summarize the best ideas?"

"Are there any especially good quotations to paste in the abstract field?

III. Sorting data

In the process of collecting data, which may arrive in graphical forms (pictures, charts and tables), as text, or as numerical tables and charts, students must begin organizing and reorganizing the data in order to find patterns and relationships. This process is the foundation for analysis and synthesis.

Key action verbs: align, arrange, array, assort, catalog, categorize, class, classify, cluster, compile, file, grade, group, layout, line up, list, order, organize, outline, pigeonhole, place, position, prioritize, program, rank, stack, tabulate. Associated tasks: bracket, collate, compare, contrast, correlate, equate, liken, match, relate.

The power of the computer becomes evident when the team of students has amassed some 500-600 forms in their database. This would be a pretty large and unmanageable stack of index cards, but when it comes time to review the information on crime, the students turn to the sorting and query tools of their database program. If they type "crime" in the resulting space, the computer locates every record containing the word "crime" and then they may sort those records by city. Finding needles is no longer so difficult.

Five students may each specialize in particular aspects of a complex research assignment yet blend their research data back into a single database, allowing for a shuffling, sorting and reshuffling of the data depending upon which question the team wishes to consider as they move past the gathering stage to the construction of insight.

The process of combining and considering findings is somewhat like weaving, embroidery, tapestry or quilting.

In the case of the New England city project, the hunters return from their trips with full sacks of "game."

Regardless of whether their information came from a book, an online periodical or the Net, they must now begin the hard work of analyzing their findings so as to compare and contrast the three cities with regard to the seven criteria mentioned at the beginning of this article (Crime-College-Sports-Parks-Shopping-Jobs-Entertainment).

IV. Analyzing data

Insight is fashioned from information. Good questions serve much like the sculptor's hands working in clay, shaping the raw material until recognizable shapes begin to emerge. Now that we have gathered several hundred records and carefully recorded them in a file, we ask, "So what? What are the implications?"

Key action verbs: The student approaches understanding - "the big picture" - by undertaking many of the following actions: clarify, interpret, construe, deduce, derive, educe, gather, glean, infer, interpret, surmise, examine, probe, and unravel.

Once the team of students has gathered 40-50 news stories, articles, statistical tables and comments regarding crime in the three New England cities, they must ask what they can "glean" from this collection of information that will guide their choice of a city.

Which city is most dangerous? Least dangerous? Is there enough difference for crime to be a deciding factor, or are all three cities nearly equivalent? Does crime emerge as a major issue, or does it drop into the background? Are there strategies (neighborhoods) which would make living in the city safe enough despite the crime rates?

Under the old research paradigm, it was enough to gather and collect. Now we place a premium on the quality of the information gathered, on the way it is organized to support reflection, and on the care with which it is analyzed.

One of the most important questions to ask during this stage is the "sufficiency" question. "Do we have enough information to proceed with our conclusions and report? Or do we need to make more visits to the Internet and the school media center to fill in the missing information?" It would be rare for most groups to move through the six stages of the Research Cycle without returning and cycling back several more times.

Conclusion

The analysis students perform during this stage of their research leads naturally to the next stage, the regrouping of information that will serve as the basis for synthesis.

Chapter 13 - Regrouping Findings

Once the students have completed their first hunting trips, gathered up fragments into carefully designed databases like those described earlier, and employed the sorting and sifting skills outlined previously, they proceed to regroup the research findings in order to make sense out of the collection. They also begin planning additional hunting trips to fill in what is missing. It is usually necessary to make several trips in order to complete the process, repeating the **Research Cycle** until sufficient relevant information has been gathered to support conclusions:

The RESEARCH CYCLE

questioning
planning
gathering
sorting & sifting
synthesizing
evaluating

       questioning
       planning
       gathering
       sorting & sifting
       synthesizing
       evaluating —————>> reporting

Regrouping Findings

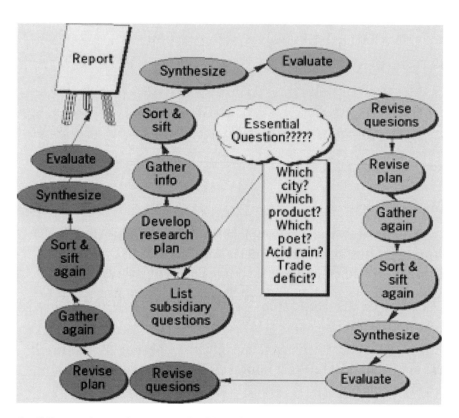

1. "Get the picture?" The Skill of SYNTHESIS

Many of us learned to put together jigsaw puzzles with an eye on the picture on the box cover. The picture we meant to assemble was clearly focused in our "mind's eye." But champion puzzlers would say that this looking at the picture is cheating. They keep it hidden, or they resort to turning the puzzle pieces upside down so that the number of clues is reduced dramatically.

Making meaning in the real world, especially in a time of turbulence and change, requires the ability to puzzle out the picture on one's own without being handed a "box cover" or picture in advance. "What do you make of that?" the group asks after gathering hundreds of fragments. They are striving for SYNTHESIS.

Smokestack schools often relied too heavily on the collection and rehashing of old insights. Students were too rarely challenged to develop their own fresh insights. Sorting and sifting through the data they have collected on the Net, they must now arrange the jigsaw pieces and fragments without ever being shown the picture. They are "on their own." They must "make up their own minds."

Picture a student or a team of students actually manipulating their fragments to see what insights might leap forth or what new ideas they might extract and create. Software programs like the electronic thesaurus and various outlining and idea processing programs may help with the visualizing and thought play. To move from information to insight, students are conjuring up new possibilities such as an array of strategies uniquely suited to protect and enhance the salmon harvest in their particular part of the Puget Sound.

In a similar manner, the team that has been working on identifying a city in New England is trying to bring each city into focus from all the bits and pieces gathered during the research. Before they can make a choice, they must make sense of the fragments. They must be able to "picture" how life might be different in each of the 5 cities being studied.

For successful synthesis to emerge, three associated levels of thinking must all occur at the same time in a dynamic, three component process that is a great deal like writing poetry or songs. All three levels operate concurrently and recursively (like the cat chasing its tail).

a. Envisioning

The top level involves conjuring and envisioning types of thought. The students conceive, conjecture, fancy, imagine, project and visualize. The students who have studied the five New England cities, for example, are now ready to write narratives describing what a typical day might be like in each city. Now that they have a pack of details and facts bundled into a database, it is time to translate them into scenarios that might help answer the question, "So what? Just how dangerous would it be to walk down those mean streets? How might it feel? Could I be proud sitting in the football stadium?"

Regrouping Findings

Envisioning is the top level because it lifts the outcomes of the research beyond past practice, antiquated mind-sets, set recipes and old thinking. The researcher leaps out of the box of everyday, ho-hum thinking.

The Internet lends itself especially well to the encouragement of such flights of fancy. The Net provides the excursions, journeys, safaris, sallies, treks and spins trainers often employ to stimulate creative problem-solving in groups. Envisioning is the source of originality. Identifying possibilities and exploring the unthinkable is basic to this level.

b. Inventing

The middle level requires translation of possibilities into actualities. The imaginative play of the top level must be grounded in reality. What might actually work? What is a sensible version of that possibility?

This is the level at which innovation is born. The student concocts new solutions to problems or coins new ideas and general principles. The research team may hatch a whole new action plan, fabricating and formulating initiatives to clean up local streams. Perhaps the thinking may advance to the development and testing of prototypes before engineering a final product.

For the team comparing and contrasting the three New England cities, they must invent pictures of their cities before they can make any kind of choice. The encyclopedia provides information about these cities, but very little of that information would shape the daily lives of our students. Their job, now that they have visited the Internet, is to construct a picture of how life with their families might play out in each setting.

c. SCAMPERING and Rearranging

The foundation for the top two levels is the rearranging mentioned earlier in this series in sections on sorting and analyzing data. A team formulating a plan to protect the salmon may take and mix up the elements from successful strategies employed to protect other endangered species. This is no time for imitating recipes of the past, in part because none of them have been fully successful. The students search for a unique plan fashioned out of old parts and new parts.

One model for such synthesis is SCAMPER, with each letter standing for a strategy.

S=substitute C=combine A=adapt M=modify, magnify, minify P=put to other uses E=eliminate R=reverse (Eberle, 1997)

For this component of synthesis to produce powerful results, the other two components - inventing and envisioning - must be operating concurrently, as they supply the pressure that inspires creation. The student arranges, blends, combines, integrates, tests, and adjusts the thought fragments until new pictures emerge and the pressure eases.

2. The Skill of EVALUATION

Seeing what's missing

"What do I know now that I didn't know then? What is it that I don't know?" When we set out to explore Essential questions like those outlined in the opening article of this series, we usually do not know enough to ask the right questions. We don't know what we don't know, so we have trouble planning our research to fill in the gaps.

Once we have visited and begun to gather fragments, our under-standing of the topic shifts and we realize we need to go back and reconsider the original research plan. As we arrange our fragments and begin to fashion meaning from what we have at hand, the shape of what is missing stands out as "negative space" just as the half-finished jigsaw puzzle hints at the shape of missing pieces.

At times, the enormity of the data cascading into our computers creates the false impression that we have fully explored some topic. Experience shows that even when we have mountains of data, we may have missed really important information. As swift as the search engines may be at locating documents, they are also quick to bypass and overlook.

The team exploring cities may have found the homicide rate for each city, for example, which would give some idea of the risk associated with living in each city. But the team has no intention of living in the whole city, so the crime rate for all of Boston doesn't tell them if they would be safe in the neighborhood they prefer. They probably need to know how many people get killed in Back Bay or the actual sections of Boston they might visit on a daily basis.

Planning further research

"What more do we need to know?" Synthesis following the first round of research is likely to leave the research group feeling unsatisfied. While the students may be approaching insight ,their understandings will remain elusive and poorly focused without repeating the Research Cycle listed at the beginning of this article:

questioning
planning
gathering
sorting & sifting
synthesizing
evaluating

Second time around, the early research efforts often provide the basis for more informed choices at the questioning and planning stages.

Scanning from the crow's nest

Maintaining perspective is paramount. While conducting research we can be trapped in the day-to-day survival activities going on at the deck level. We are too close to the action to see the patterns in it. "Climbing the mast" means stepping outside and above the activities to see them with some distance and perspective. The crow's nest allows one to look beyond the ship to ask questions about the challenges and goals that lie ahead. It means keeping the big picture and the essential questions in mind.

Each research team needs to step out of the activities periodically and ask a few questions. "How are we doing? Is our plan working?

Regrouping Findings

Do we need to shift strategies? Change our focus? Ask different questions? Consider different sources?"

Conclusion

The research experience is rarely as linear as various models may suggest. It is probable that groups will "go around in circles" before arriving at the insight level. The first attempts at synthesis will almost always provoke additional questions and additional research. As the gaps in the jigsaw puzzle drive the inquiry, the group will return again and again until they have enough information to formulate a report. The next chapter will examine the final stages of the **Research Cycle**, as students move from information to insight to persuasion.

Chapter 14 - Information to Persuasion

After passing through several repetitions of the **Research Cycle** as outlined in the preceding chapters, a student or team of students will eventually determine that they have established a sufficient basis for insight. Having devoted long hours to the collection, sorting and sifting of data, they are now ready to answer the question, "So what?" And they are ready to provide at least tentative answers to the original essential questions that provoked the research project in the first place.

For the team seeking ways of protecting the salmon (as well as the fishing folk, the timber people and the utilities), it is now time to outline and present a set of action recommendations. The presentation must be illuminating (as in "casting light" upon the subject), but it must also be persuasive. If we set up such projects properly, the report is presented to an authentic audience such as a state legislator or to a mixed group of special interest representatives whose behaviors the students hope to influence.

For the team selecting a New England city, it is now time to present their findings to their parents in a way that will establish the case for the winning city. This does not mean a "skewed" or a "slanted" case. The team must fairly report the pros and cons of each city in terms of the selection criteria established early in the project, but they must do so in a clear, highly compacted manner that allows the parents to see the evidence without actually having to wade through all of it.

From Information to Persuasion

1. The Old Report

"How long does this have to be?"

There was a time - not so long ago, actually -when some teachers attached minimum length requirements to papers and reports, as if length were directly related to adequacy and quality of thought. Of course, most of these reports were topical in nature, requiring "information-moving machines" like the building-sized equipment we see pictured in quarries. The idea was to gather as much information about a country or state or city as one could in one month's time and then lay out paragraph after paragraph of badly twisted prose produced by changing one word in each sentence. Length was associated with adequacy of coverage.

2. The New Report

"What shall we do?"

Students can now download hundreds of pages of articles and text without ever really reading them, understanding them or synthesizing them. Information has become so generally and abundantly available that students are confronted with a veritable "groaning board" of items, much of which is not much better than "fast food." In a time of "infoglut" it makes little sense to judge the quality of research by the number of pages submitted. To the contrary, it may be time to strictly limit the number of words and pages presented.

If research has focused upon the kinds of essential questions suggested by this book, the final report or presentation may suggest action of some kind. "What shall we do?" Decision-making and problem-solving both require a reasonable choice from a list of options. It is the job of the research team to distill their findings until they are sharing the most cogent and compelling information.

Cogent? The research team asks whether the information being shared with their audience is to the point, well-grounded, well-argued, well-put, and relevant.

From Information to Persuasion

President Reagan was fond of requiring single page action recommendations from his cabinet, even when the decision was exceedingly complex. Even though his enemies suggested that his mind could not handle more complexity, there was wisdom in his strategy. Behind the summary page lay far more information. He wished to move straight to the "heart of the matter."

3. The New Report - Elements

"The sum of the parts."

The new school report contains the following elements:

• The consideration of a complex, essential question requiring either decision-making or problem-solving.

The emphasis of this process is the construction and reporting of new understandings. The performance by the students is intended to enlighten the audience, to open their minds to new ways of thinking. If they do their jobs well, they will educate!

• A team effort.

Complex questions require a team to split up the work load, with each member taking on responsibility for major sections of the research plan described in the first article of this series. Practice in such teaming is directly relevant to the workplace skills most of our students will be asked to wield when solving problems for their future employers.

• A clear explanation of the team's recommendations and conclusions.

The team sums up its position in a few tersely worded sentences that have been stripped of unnecessary language. This statement should be short, emphatic and precise.

• An economical summary of the findings used to support and sustain the recommendations.

The team should identify and serve up just that evidence and information that is most compelling. Given the mountains and gigabits of data teams can collect with new technologies, this selection process is like sharing the tip of an iceberg. Just as statisticians speak of "crunching the numbers" to capture the idea of extracting meaning from thousands and thousands of data points, the research team presses the textual information they have gathered into something intense and fine.

• Supporting data and information stored in searchable formats.

The rest of the data is still valuable, but it may be submitted as a database. The group can easily demonstrate that it has hundreds of files to back up its position. They need not actually show up as printed pages. The teacher may scan the records as part of the evaluation. It is also possible for the group to employ hyperlinked text to present findings in multilayered files. The top layers provide the focus for the performance. The middle and lower layers offer opportunities to examine data and evidence in far more detail and depth.

• The skillful use of presentation technologies of various kinds to maximize persuasiveness.

Programs like **Persuasion, PowerPoint, HyperCard**, and **HyperStudio** support multimedia presentations that allow students to employ an impressive array of tools to make their case. The students may apply sound, motion, still photographs, graphs, tables and hyperlinked text to the challenge of educating and persuading the audience. The simple text-based report of yesteryear still has an important place as supportive information.

• Evidence of logical reasoning.

In the old report, gathering a large quantity of information was the priority. In the new report, demonstrating powerful reasoning is the priority. The argument (or case) should be laid out by the research team in a clear, highly structured manner.

4. Evaluating the New Report

As with most school work, students deserve to be told the evaluation criteria before they begin work on the project. As the team moves through the stages of the **Research Cycle**, the teacher holds structured conferences with the group every few days to monitor progress, make suggestions, provoke questions, and provide evaluative feedback.

In order to stress the importance of the research "process," it makes good sense to award credit and make evaluative grades of some sort for performance at each stage using rubrics like those offered in The Oak Harbor Information Skills Rating Form. (http://fno.org/libskill.html) Teachers too often save their grading for the end product.

Sample Criteria for Planning and Hunting Stages

How well does each student:

Question - employ questions to identify what the team needs to learn?

Categorize - break down and rearrange the thinking of the group into related groupings?

Suggest - offer ideas, strategies and direction?

Listen - build and support - piggyback, encourage, elaborate, ask for clarification?

Map - organize concepts, questions and challenges visually?

Sample Criteria for Sorting, Sifting and Synthesizing Stages

How well does each student:

Organize - set up and utilize categories to support sorting and sifting.

Rearrange - move information fragments around and test intriguing combinations.

Listen, build and support - piggyback, encourage, elaborate, ask for clarification?

Challenge - test the quality of thinking, push the investigation, review the logic, ask the unquestionable.

Assess - weigh the adequacy, the cogency, and the coherence of the case.

From Information to Persuasion

Sample Criteria for Reporting

How well does each student:

Summarize - select and condense critical concepts, findings, and evidence.

Organize - arrange the core material in a coherent, logical manner.

Present - exploit the array of multimedia tools available to "lay out" the case in a thorough and effective manner.

Persuade - make a connection with the passions and the interests of the audience in order to gain support for a particular recommendation or position.

Conclusion

So little school research seemed to matter to students. Many of us were caught up in a ritual that was hard on both students and teachers. I can recall my own first years of teaching and the agony I sometimes inspired in the name of research. The country reports were probably the worst. Information moved from page to page, but insight was rarely a product.

Research should matter to our students. They should care about the outcomes. They should feel passionately about the discoveries. Now and again they should thrill to an authentic "Aha!" or "Eureka!"

The ultimate test of our success is whether the students themselves can answer the question, "So what?" Did all the investigating lead to discoveries and insights that will illuminate their lives? Did they emerge with skills that will serve them well in their futures as family members, citizens and workers grappling with the issues and problems of the next century?

Chapter 15 - Searching for the Grail

Power Searching with Digital Logic

No sense sending students and colleagues out to search the Internet or a CD-ROM encyclopedia unless they possess a toolkit of powerful search strategies to speed them past Infoglut and Info-Garbage to the very information they need.

Power Searching cuts past what David Shenk calls "Data Smog."

Learn these ten strategies and you are on your way to information that is pertinent, cogent and worth saving. Converting such information into insight requires a different set of strategies.

1. Question and draw before grazing
2. Use only the best
3. Learn the syntax
4. Learn the features
5. Start big and broad
6. Browse before search
7. Go to the source
8. Be discrete
9. Cull your findings
10. Be playful

Searching for the Grail

Search engines don't work well on the almost unlimited, often unstructured resources of the Internet, says J. Pemberton:

> Think of a search engine as a dog whistle. Blow it in a kennel and you'll just attract dogs. Blow it in a zoo, and you'll get a few dogs, plus many other creatures with good high frequency hearing: maybe some lions or tigers, hyenas, coyotes, timber wolves, perhaps a moose. . . . The point is this: the Internet is a zoo.
>
> Jeffrey K. Pemberton's column
> **Online User Magazine**, May/June 1996.

1. Question and draw before you search

Think and draw before you plunge. Make a list of great questions. Take advantage of Mindware like Inspiration to create a cluster diagram with several dozen concepts, keywords and telling questions which will be powerfully instrumental later when executing your search.

You might ask your students to work as teams to propose a mix of laws and government programs which would serve to protect old growth forests while restoring the vitality of this nation's timber industry.

You send them to one particularly intriguing article to start them thinking. You ask them to work in teams to create cluster diagrams listing as many pertinent concepts and keywords as possible.

One team's diagram looks something like the figure on the facing page.

You also send students to the electronic thesaurus to make sure they have a full listing of suitable search terms. They may begin their research with a seriously limited grasp of the major concepts and terms employed by those knowledgeable in the field under study. Without knowing these terms they are likely to find writing that has been done by the amateurs and the lay people. A strong grasp of vocabulary improves the success of word searching.

Searching for the Grail

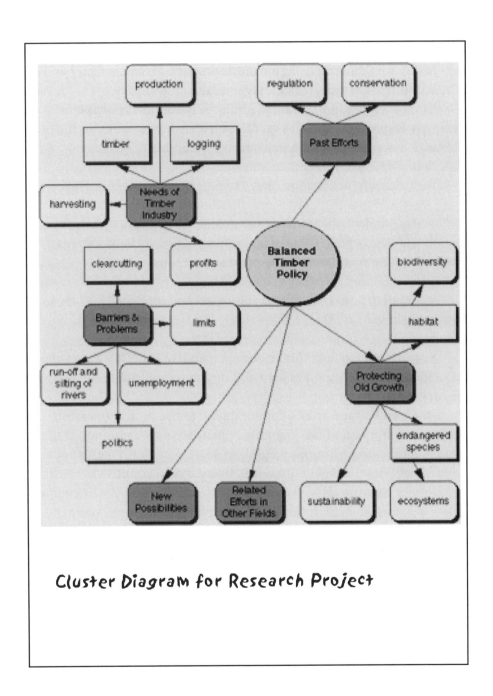

Cluster Diagram for Research Project

Searching for the Grail

2. Use only the best

Pick the best search engine. Bookmark it.

Stay with that search engine until someone invents a faster and better information trap (which may not take long).

Do not rely upon the "search" buttons built into **Netscape** or **Internet Explorer**. These lists create advertising revenue for the software companies and the placement of search engines may be a function of revenue rather than value.

How do you pick a good one? Two basic strategies:

1. Read independent reviews, valuable for the way they look at search engines as well as the actual ratings. An excellent source of reviews can be found at http://www.searchenginewatch.com/

2. Conduct your own evaluation based on criteria such as those offered below.

Speed - How quickly do pages open and how swiftly do results of searches appear? Some search engines are graphically (advertising) bloated.

Boolean Capabilities - Learning how to use logical operators such as AND, OR and NOT greatly enhances your searching. If the search engine doesn't support Boolean searching, don't waste your time. Fuzzy Logic usually produces fuzzy search results.

Power Sorting & Searching Features - The best search engines allow you to sort and sift findings by dates, type of page, type of domain (.com vs. .edu), etc.

Interface Design - Good search engines keep the search box front and center where you can enter words without scrolling about. How well are the items and choices laid out on the page? Can you find what you need when and where you need it? Do ads get in the way of your searching?

Browsing Capabilities - Can you look at more than 10 "hits" at a time? It is very helpful to quickly scan the first 100 hits. Is the description or annotation of each item sufficient to provide a basis for making a wise choice? Can you determine relevancy?

Breadth & Depth of Database - Some search engines and their spiders do a better job of collecting from the world's vast array of Web sites. Is larger better?

Digital Logic - Many search engines employ artificial intelligence and digital logic to determine relevancy, proximity and other issues which might help you find the best information. Do they explain the rules of their system or are they hidden? When Web sites and pages appear in the top 20, do they actually belong there?

Reasonable Advertising - Some search engines accept advertising which might offend. Do you care? If so, which seem OK to you?

Useful Results - The bottom line or essential question is "How useful are the results?" Do you find reliable and relevant information swiftly?

No matter which search engine you select, do not settle for the "simple search" version of any. You are sacrificing power and accuracy for ease of use. It's a bit like training wheels on a bike. Go for the Power Search or the Advanced Search and encourage your students to do the same. They offer features that will vastly improve your results when combined with the suggestion in this article.

3. Learn the syntax

The more powerful the search engine, the more important the syntax - the rules governing how you enter your search query. Because few people stop to read and learn these rules, they sometimes end up with crude or clumsy searches.

For example, some search engines care about CAPITAL LETTERS and punctuation. Others ignore them both. If you search for Washington, D.C. with the following query, you may achieve no "hits" with one search engine and thousands with another.

WASHINGTON, DC

Another example: when you want an exact phrase such as "old

growth forest," some search engines require quotation marks around the words that belong together, while others do not care.

Another example: when you are conducting Boolean searches, some search engines require that you capitalize AND, OR and NOT. Failure to do so may convince your search engine to ignore these critical words.

You can usually find the syntax for any search engine in the Help pages. If not, you may want to look for an engine that explains its rules.

4. Learn the features

As Infoglut has grown to be more and more of a problem, the search engines have competed fiercely to offer the best tools to support you in your sorting and sifting, and yet I have witnessed hundreds of folks ignoring these powerful extra tools and features.

HotBot's Super Search allows you to request particular domains, particular dates, particular levels of a Web site, particular countries of origin, particular types of files and as many as 100 results at a time. These can be very helpful search features.

The Power Searcher explores all of the features of a chosen search engine in advance of real searching in order to apply these extra tools with skill when they are needed.

5. Start big and broad (then narrow cautiously)

Effective searching requires a balance between a broad reach and a careful aim. The searcher must cast a net far enough to capture the most important information, and then, once safely contained, must cull the results so that only the best information remains.

Our first search for "old growth forest" produces more than 5,000 hits, many of which are irrelevant. When we browse through the findings, we see that these 5600 hits fall into major categories related to forest, habitat, ecosystem, lands, conservation, wildlife, etc. Since we are just beginning our exploration, we may want to conduct fresh searches for each of these concepts to see what other ideas, issues and possibilities are associated with our original search phrase.

Too many searchers narrow their searches prematurely, thereby condemning themselves to the boundaries and ideas of their prior knowledge.

Most of us do not understand the forest of our question well enough at this stage to start looking at individual trees and bark and leaves.

This is the time to map out the territory into conceptual zones, each of which becomes a neighborhood worthy of more carefully focused exploration.

If we have little prior knowledge of "sustainability" we could not know what we do not know and could not plan or pose the questions we ought to be exploring. We might learn some before we focus narrowly and sharply.

6. Browse before grazing

Early search efforts are meant to provide an overview of the information landscape relevant to the investigation at hand, much like petroleum prospectors flying over a region and noting the terrain, seeking convergence (a combination of geological elements in one location which hints at the presence of oil).

While it is tempting to start right off opening pages and looking for information, it is more effective to wait until you have scanned the brief descriptions most search engines provide for the hits. Scanning the top 100 hits provides a basis for revising the original search to accomplish two goals:

1. Exclude whole categories of irrelevant sites

2. Target more directly those pages and sites most likely to deliver a great return

Think of the first search as a potluck supper with a 400 foot long table. Would you step up to the very first dish and start heaping food onto your plate? Or would you browse and graze before making choices?

Searching for the Grail

7. Go to the source

Some of the best sites on the Internet are not indexed by the search engines. It pays to go to such Web sites and search them directly if they would be the leading source of information on a particular topic.

One outstanding example would be the huge collection of educational research documents housed at ERIC (http://ericir.syr.edu/). If you perform a search for "middle school guidance" on the free Internet, you are unlikely to find much worth reading (a mere 195 hits with Altavista), while ERIC provides hundreds of abstracts of research articles from several decades.

It turns out that because many public agencies and news media Web sites do not permit access (perhaps for security reasons) to the spiders of search engines, their contents often elude the search engine's efforts as well as our own search attempts.

If you know that the **New York Times**, the **Wall Street Journal**, the **Seattle Times** and the **Los Angeles Times** have all been giving careful attention to a recent lawsuit such as the Justice Department suit against Microsoft, you may achieve far better results by starting your search at their Web sites rather than wasting time with a global search engine which would overlook their offerings.

After several years of looking for a good source of crime statistics using global search engines, I came to realize that I would have done better if I had started with the source, the Federal Bureau of Justice (http://www.usdoj.gov/), a site which never showed up when I would use global search strategies.

What is the best way to know what source or Web site to visit?

• Make a list of organizations most likely to care enough about your question, issue or topic to gather and share information about it. Visit their Web sites and see what they have to offer.

• Consult one or more of the printed Internet guides that often suggest the best sites for various subject areas such as Civil War Photographs (Library of Congress). Kathy Schrock's **Guide for Educators** is one of the best.

Searching for the Grail

http://discoveryschool.com/schrockguide/).

• Take advantage of an index or directory such as Yahoo (http://www.yahoo.com) to see which sites offer information on a particular subject.

• Ask a good librarian.

8. Be discrete

After you have conducted several browsing searches, you may begin to focus your search more sharply by adding key words to your search in order to limit hits to pages distinctly relevant to your inquiry.

Careful selection and addition of key words that are discriminating, distinguishing and distinctive, puts the spotlight on just those discrete pages which match your interests. Your key words differentiate, separate and reserve only the best pages.

How different would your results be with each of the following words?

• owl (156,000 hits)
• spotted owl (7,385 hits)
• marbled owl

The more you particularize your search, the better your results. Adding particulars and specifics excludes all pages that do not contain those items. The advantage is sharp focus. The danger is bypassing, missing or overlooking key data.

Sometimes it pays to alternate between narrowing and broadening. After zeroing in with some particulars, zoom back out and try some different particulars.

This may also be a good time to use wild cards, truncation, the logical operator "OR" and "exact phrase" syntax.

9. Cull your findings

The most powerful strategy for culling your original findings is the use of the logical operator "NOT" - which may be AND NOT in some search engines (Altavista).

127

Searching for the Grail

As you browse the first 100 hits, look for patterns and groupings of irrelevant pages. In order to exclude all such irrelevant pages from your collection, add AND NOT with a series of key words contained within parentheses and divided by OR.

If you search for "Mayflower" do you really want all the motels, hotels, insurance companies and moving companies? If not, try the following search:

Mayflower AND NOT (motels OR hotels OR insurance companies OR moving companies)

10. Be playful

Power Searching is often more successful when you listen to your intuition and take chances. If you enjoy word play, you will have good luck with the trial-and-error searching process that leads to good results. Listen to your hunches. Be a Sherlock Holmes or Nancy Drew. Don't be so analytical and logical that you cannot make intuitive leaps. Digital logic is the attempt to find order in an erratic, chaotic and disorganized information landscape.

Chapter 16 - The New Plagiarism

Introduction

Could electronic text spawn a virulent strain of student copying? Is cut-and-paste the enemy of thought? Many teachers who work in "wired schools" are complaining that new technologies have made it all too easy for students to gather the ideas of others and present them as their own.

A **New York Times** article reported in September of 1998 that "cheating is on the rise." The New Plagiarism may be worse than the old because students now wield an **electronic shovel** that makes it possible to find and save huge chunks of information with little reading, effort or originality.

Is the New Plagiarism any worse than the old?

Under the old system of "go find out about" topical research, it took students a huge amount of time to move words from the encyclopedia pages onto white index cards, changing one word in each sentence so as to avoid plagiarism.

The New Plagiarism requires little effort and is geometrically more powerful. While the pre-modem student might misappropriate a dozen ideas from a handful of thinkers, the post-modem student can download and save hundreds of pages per hour. We have moved from the horse and buggy days of plagiarism to the Space Age without stopping for the horseless carriage.

As this chapter will point out, it is reckless and irresponsible to continue requiring topical, "go find out about" research projects in this new electronic context. To do so extends an invitation to "binge" on mere information gathering.

We have more to worry about here than the Web sites offering term papers for sale (visit WWW.A1-Termpaper.Com) or the sites that offer assistance with college essays. What we have is a societal shift toward glib and facile understandings allied with an archaic school research program (in some places) that places little value upon questioning and original thought.

The seven antidotes offered below are intended to cut off this new strain of plagiarism before it becomes an academic plague.

Antidote 1
Distinguish between levels and types of research.

In moving beyond the topical research that has held students back for so long, we must help all teachers and students to see the difference between three levels of research and help them to see the value (even necessity) of playing down the first two levels in favor of the third.

Level One Research "Just the Facts"

In these kinds of projects and quests, the student is expected to gather basic facts and information about a state or a city or a country or a battle or a general or a writer or a scientist. Little thinking is required. This is information gathering at its crudest and simplest level. Everybody needs to learn how to find specific facts for specific purposes, but we need to make sure school research goes further.

The New Plagiarism

Level Two Research - "Other People's Ideas"

Even though these kinds of projects may engage students in considering important questions such as the causes of acid rain or overpopulation, it is sufficient for the student to gather "conventional thinking" and the best ideas of others. These are the research projects most likely to inspire plagiarism as the student gathers other people's ideas and then passes them off as her or his own.

We certainly want students to familiarize themselves with the wisdom of the ages, but we don't want them to stop there or accept conventional wisdom without question.

Level Three Research - "In My Humble Opinion"

When we require fresh thinking, we stand the least risk of suborning plagiarism. If students cannot find the answers but must make the answers, they are less apt to pass off others' ideas as their own. The secret is to pose or ask students to pose questions or problems and decisions that have never been adequately answered.

"How do we restore peace to Northern Ireland?"

Antidote 2 - Discourage "trivial pursuits."

Even though students must learn how to find discrete facts such as the population of Chile or France, we have labored too long in those vineyards.

We need fewer treasure and scavenger hunts.

One student sent me an e-mail asking for the number of gargoyles on the Cathedral of Notre Dame in Paris. This was an extra credit assignment from her teacher who took some pride in no student having ever answered the question successfully.

Trivial pursuit? Why not ask an important, thought provoking question about gargoyles, instead?

"Why do people put gargoyles on churches and office buildings?

131

The New Plagiarism

What good are they?"

The student showed great resourcefulness using the Net to find people who might know something about gargoyles, but I only had photographs of gargoyles on my Web site and could not provide the answer. In subsequent research it turned out that no one may know the correct answer. Not only trivial but unanswerable?

It is time to emphasize questions that challenge students at the top of Bloom's Taxonomy.

We launch projects that require:

- Explanations
- Problem-solving
- Choices & Decision-Making

We build our programs around the "Prime Questions"

Why
How
Which is best?

We transform topical research into projects that demand that students move past mere gathering of information to the construction of new meanings and insight.

Example: Instead of asking why events turned out particular ways in our past (a question fraught with plagiaristic opportunities since historians have probably already offered answers), we might ask students to hypothesize why various outcomes did not occur.

Example: Instead of asking how we might protect an endangered species whose chances have already been improved (the bald eagle), we might focus on one which no one has managed to protect (various Australian marsupials, for example).

Example: Instead of asking students to study a single country or city, we might ask them to decide which is best for various purposes (the Winter Olympics, a university degree, the building of a theme park, etc.).

The New Plagiarism

Students become producers of insight and ideas rather than mere consumers.

Antidote 3.
Emphasize Essential Questions.

Essential questions are questions worth asking, questions that touch upon basic human issues or touch matters of the heart and the soul. Often as not, they spawn inquiries that might extend over a month or a lifetime. - investigations that might make a difference in the quality of life - studies that might cast light in dark corners, illuminating basic truths.

These essential questions are not immune to plagiarism, since the world's greatest thinkers may have "had their turn" at proposing answers, but combined with the next three antidotes, they can be quite effective as inspiration for originality.

Antidote 4.
Require and enable students to make their own answers.

We need to ask students to make up their own minds and do their own thinking. But first schools must do a far better job of equipping students with questioning skills as well as a strong foundation in Synthesis (the process of altering and modifying the elements of anything until it has been significantly changed or improved).

Synthesis can be taught. Note the emphasis upon synthesis in Chapter Thirteen of this book.

While some claim that, "There are no new ideas under the sun," our students must learn how to apply some extra color or tone it down. They must learn to see the underlying structure and then construct or deconstruct the original until it shimmers with originality.

These are the same inferential reasoning skills that many states are beginning to require as part of their demanding state standards.

The New Plagiarism

Antidote 5
Focus upon systematic storage.

We expect students to keep pertinent information only. And we want them to be planning ahead for retrieval at a later stage. We also hope to monitor the gathering process from beginning to end.

"How can I organize my findings so I can make sense of them later on?"

Information in electronic forms is much easier to store and organize for later review than printed material. As much as possible we want our students to know how to take notes electronically, cutting and pasting when appropriate, paraphrasing when desirable. We also want them to be able to search their findings months later with some efficiency and power.

Students are extracting, paraphrasing, summarizing and extending the information they have found with eyes directly focused upon the essential question. At the same time, they are citing the source of their information and ideas.

The information will be more valuable later if it sits within the computer rather than being buried in a pile of hundreds of pages of printed material.

We show students how to take notes with a database program.

A standard format may look something like this, but students may tailor it to fit the subject.

Source: (Author, Title, Date, URL)
Subject:
Keywords:
Abstract:

The New Plagiarism

Subject Words

It pays to teach your students how to develop a relatively brief list of subject words drawn from their cluster diagram. In order to show them the power of a well constructed database, you should give them a chance to explore the searching capabilities of one you have constructed. Show them how subject words support the sorting and sifting that will later help them make meaning of their findings.

If we were comparing three cities, for example, we might use crime, weather, shopping and employment along with each city's name as subject words.

Keywords

Demonstrate for your students that keywords offer a greater level of detail and work at the sub category level below subject words.

If we were researching crime (from above) in three cities, for example, we might use "statistics," "murder," "trends," "violent," "prevention" and "property" as keywords.

Abstract

The abstract is where students save pertinent information. We must teach them to paraphrase and condense, avoiding the cutting and pasting of huge (often unread) blocks of text.

Antidote 6.
Stress "green ink" and citation ethics.

If we hope to witness our students producing fresh thinking, then we need to award credit for smart collecting but also show them how to differentiate between the ideas they have collected from others and those ideas that have emerged in reaction to the ideas of others.

They may change colors or type styles while note-taking to signify and separate their own ideas from others.

Black text signifies the ideas of others.
Green text (or bold text) signifies fresh thinking.

The New Plagiarism

We award credit for originality, noting each new contribution.
For example:

> **Source:** May, 1998, From Now On, Jamie McKenzie,
> "The New Plagiarism: Seven Antidotes to Prevent High-
> way Robbery in an Electronic Age." http://fno.org/
> may98/cov98may.html
> **Subject:** research, plagiarism, strategies
> **Keywords:** incentives, rewards
> **Abstract:** McKenzie suggests the use of green ink to help
> student differentiate between the ideas they have collected
> and the new ideas they have built in reaction to those
> inspirations. **Reminds me a bit of art with "found
> objects." Here we have "found ideas" and "fresh
> ideas." I like students having to keep them separate. I
> could then look over their shoulders while they did
> research to see what kinds of balance might emerge. It
> might change how I did assessment?**

The teacher acts like a "guide on the side" acknowledging the
good new ideas as they appear on the screen.

Antidote 7
Assess progress throughout the entire research process.

If we seek an end to plagiarism, then we keep an eye on the note-
taking and idea development as they evolve. We encourage, we
provide nudges, we congratulate and we (occasionally) light fires. We
do not wait until the end to let our students know how they are doing.

More importantly, we provide clear rubrics for valued behaviors
so that students make take a hand at self-assessment.

We may use the **Multimedia Rubrics** available from ISTE.

The New Plagiarism

http://www2.ncsu.edu/ncsu/cep/midlink/rub.multi.htm
Or we may use the **Oak Harbor Information Skills Rubrics**.
http://fno.org/libskill.html

One part of the Oak Harbor Rubrics is shown below:

Building Upon Others' Ideas
A researcher reads with the intent of extending and augmenting the ideas of others.
5 - Pushes "found ideas" well beyond their original boundaries
3 - Adjusts and elaborates upon "found ideas"
1 - Translates and summarizes without adding

A strong commitment to ongoing assessment that emphasizes the importance of original thought can provide a powerful incentive to minimize plagiarism.

Part Three

Research Cycles & Scaffolding

Chapter 17 - Building Research Modules

A productive way to build research modules is to call a team of teachers together with a strong media specialist or teacher librarian at a time of year when they are already feeling overwhelmed by the "daily press" of teaching. Summer is best. Extra pay is essential.

The team may include a mixture of late adopting, skeptical teachers along with early adopting enthusiasts so that the school attains "convergence" - the drawing together of groups that don't always see "eye to eye" on important matters.

This chapter outlines the steps of the invention process in a manner that parallels the steps described online in Module-Maker at http://questioning.org/module/module.html. A similar process may be employed to construct WebQuests, directions for which may be found online at http://edweb.sdsu.edu/webquest/webquest.html

Building Research Modules

Stage One - Re-Thinking
Questions, Questioning & Research

Because most of us grew up with a firm grounding in topical research, it is essential that an invention team take the time to read through sections on essential questions (Chapters Two and Three) so that all members are clear about what we mean by research requiring fresh thought.

There is an ever present danger that team members will revert to traditional school research patterns that only ask students to gather information instead of pondering challenging questions. Each team member should spend at least an hour reading about essential questions and then should join in a discussion of how these parallel the kinds of questions now appearing on state and provincial tests.

Before the exploration and construction stages begin, each member of the invention team must acknowledge the value of moving away from old fashioned research rituals, and they must have a clear sense that research modules will require students to make up their own minds about a decision, an issue or a problem.

Stage Two - Considering the Traits of Research Modules

1. A question requiring original thought

Each research module engages students in as many as 3-10 classroom periods worth of exploration. They will be making a choice based on a careful comparing and contrasting of several options or they may be solving a problem by coming up with some novel strategies never tried previously. This is not topical research. Much of the effort will be devoted to thinking and puzzling. Each research module is focused on an essential question - one worthy of consideration and deep thought.

Building Research modules

2. A clear sequence of steps

As was outlined extensively in Chapter 16, scaffolding is extensive throughout a research module, with examples accompanying detailed, clear instructions. An effective research module offers all eight of the advantages attributed to scaffolding (clear directions, clarity of purpose, pointers to resources, clear expectations, assessment rubrics, efficiency, momentum and on task behavior.)

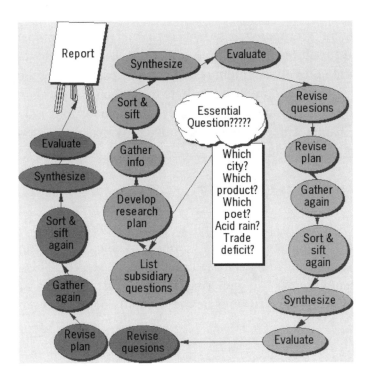

3. Use of the Research Cycle

Research modules are built in a series of Web "pages" that are linked together much like beads on a string. They follow the stages outlined in Chapter Eight - "The Research Cycle." Students move from questioning to planning, from gathering to sorting and sifting, from synthesis to evaluation, and then are likely to repeat the cycle several times as their research feeds them new questions and awakens them to the dimensions of a research challenge. Each time they reach the evaluation stage, they ask if they have developed enough understanding to stop gathering information and move on the reporting/ persuading stage.

4. Selective gathering

Research modules emphasize the importance of holding onto just the most pertinent information. Students are given many graphical organizers and structures to focus their selection. The goal is to teach them to hold onto only those findings that actually cast light on the information challenge and might contribute to the final decision or challenge. Key to this strategy is the use of "telling questions" as explained in Chapter Three. Students are also provided explicit instructions regarding note-taking.

5. Expanded questioning

Research modules require students to "look before they leap" - expecting students to make a major investment in cluster diagramming the many subsidiary questions that will guide their research. This expanded questioning prior to gathering helps increase their devotion to the most pertinent information once they actually begin their gathering.

6. Ongoing assessment

Assessment begins during the first module of a research module and continues on throughout the research process. Students are shown rubrics at the beginning of the project and are expected to join in the assessment process with the teacher, sharing responsibility for assessing and adjusting the quality of work.

Building Research Modules

7. Multiple Sources - Pre-Selected

While it is fashionable today for students to plunge into electronic sources - especially the Internet - without much thought about the desirability of various sources, research modules often encourage the use of books, CD-ROMs, online subscriptions and sources in addition to the Internet, knowing that good research is often best served by these other media.

Research modules are built with profound respect for the continuing value of books and libraries.

In addition, when they do use the Internet, most research modules steer students toward sites that offer reliability, authority, accuracy and organization. The inventors usually spend hours sifting through hundreds of worthless sites in order to find those most suitable for the curriculum goals and age levels of the students.

8. Team research

In keeping with the tenets of **Engaged Learning (Plugging In**, 1995), students are expected to conduct research as partners in a team enterprise, working together to explore an issue, gather pertinent information, test out new ideas and formulate a decision or solution.

Engaged Learning calls for students to work collaboratively and strategically. Students are responsible for their own learning while energized by a challenging question. The parallels with workplace skills and expectations are clear as employees frequently find themselves working on teams (often remotely) to develop new products and new ways of doing things.

9. Repeated attempts at synthesis

Coming up with fresh answers to difficult questions is no simple task. Research modules presume that students must try and then try again, that they will arrange and rearrange their findings until some kind of picture begins to emerge, until some semblance of meaning takes form. First efforts will often suggest the need for further re-search and further thought.

Unless students are urged to stop in the middle of gathering and urged to "take stock" of their findings, they can easily fall into an activity trap. Gathering can proceed without much strategy. By stopping to reflect, students

10. Multimedia presentation or an authentic performance

Many research modules encourage students to make use of pre-sentation software such as **PowerPoint** or **HyperStudio**, but there is some growing concern that such presentations can be heavy on glitter while light on content and rigor. Many teachers are turning to some blend of traditional paper backed by some kind of multimedia presen-tation. The goal is to provide students with opportunities to share their findings and their ideas with real audiences whenever possible.

As explained in Chapter Fifteen, students provide a clear explana-tion of the team's recommendations and conclusions. The team sums up its position in a few tersely worded sentences that have been stripped of unnecessary language. This statement should be short, emphatic and precise. They also include an economical summary of the findings used to support and sustain their recommendations.

The team should identify and serve up just that evidence and information that is most compelling.

Stage Three - Exploring Models

After a solid grounding in questioning and the traits of research modules, the team moves on to visit and consider the attributes of projects built by teachers from schools around the world. By evaluat-ing the work of other teachers, the team begins to develop a personal definition of an effective research module.

For each project visited, teachers enter comments in a word processing file with three columns:

Building Research Modules

Pro	Con	Interesting

They will find examples in the following locations:

Baltimore County Maryland
http://www.bcpl.net/~sullivan/modules

Bateman's Bay, New South Wales, Australia
http://www.cap.nsw.edu.au/bb_site_intro/bbcap_intro.html

Bellingham, Washington
Fifth grade science (Planets)
http://wwwsil.bham.wednet.edu/Curriculum/paBASECAMP.HTM
Fifth grade social studies (Explorers)
http://wwwsil.bham.wednet.edu/Curriculum/homeport.htm

Grand Prairie ISD Texas
http://www.gpisd.org/gpisd/modules/modulepage.html

After several hours of exploration, the group reconvenes and trades stories and reactions, pointing out which features seemed most effective, which ones were disconcerting or problematical and which features are missing. Most groups will be eager to begin their own modules now that they have spent time visiting and exploring.

Stage Four - Saving and Re-Naming Templates

In most cases, teams will arrive with much experience or skill when it comes to Web page construction. The best strategy is to begin all module construction in a word processing program such as **Word** or **AppleWorks**, both of which can easily be translated into HTML (Web) pages at a later date.

Building Research modules

Before progressing any further, each team should open up each of the template pages provided with **Module Maker** at http://questioning.org/module/module6.html

Visit One	Questioning and Planning
Visit Two	Gathering/Sorting/Sifting 1
Visit Three	Gathering/Sorting/Sifting 2
Visit Four	Synthesis - Time to stop and "take inventory."
	• Which questions are well answered?
	• Which ones require further investigation?
	• Any new questions?
Visit Five	Gathering/Sorting/Sifting 3
Visit Six	Synthesis
Visit Seven	Presentation

They should open each template with their browser (Netscape or Internet Explorer) and then SAVE AS (text) with a series of file names such as lesson1, lesson2, lesson3, lesson 4. If the team has HTML skills, they may save these templates as SOURCE.

In either case, the files, once saved, will be reopened with a word processing or HTML editing program and modified to match the team's intentions, preferences and style.

The templates are meant only to offer suggestions and guidance. They should not be viewed as some kind of strait jacket or set of serious limitations. They point out activities, elements and content that might be useful to many teams.

Stage Five - Identifying Promising Questions

Finding a wonderful unit question can be the most difficult task for most invention teams. It may also be the most important.

Once the team has fixed upon a dramatic choice or problem drawn from the curriculum, the rest of the research module seems to fall into place without much real difficulty. On the other hand, teams that have difficulty identifying a question at the top of Bloom's **Tax-**

onomy often flounder and experience frustration.

There are many demanding questions that teams might explore, but for those without great experience building curriculum units around essential questions, the safest route to a good question is to find a choice or a problem.

"Which of these three inventions had the most impact? Why?"

"Which of these three writers had the most powerful style? Why?"

"What should we do to reduce the poverty of our cities?"

"What should we do to reduce the pollution in our streams?"

"What should we do to make the Internet a safe place for students?"

The best strategy is to brainstorm 3-6 good questions at this stage and then spend some time prospecting during the next stage to determine whether or not there are sufficient resources available, electronically and in print, to support the kind of quality research effort the team expects.

In a surprisingly large percentage of cases, teams discover that great questions are not necessarily well matched by great information resources.

Stage Six - Prospecting to Cull Promising Questions

The most efficient way to determine which of the first 3-6 questions might be worthy of a full blown research module is to split up the team into pairs and let each pair test the information available for 1-2 questions.

It usually takes less than an hour to discover which of the initial list is worth pursuing. In some rare cases (especially when the focus is upon history and the humanities), the team may have to create a new list of questions, but usually they will find at least one question that holds promise.

Building Research Modules

Stage Seven - Writing Directions

Once the team has settled upon a question, it must be written precisely and clearly in the file for the first module. The team must remember the reading level of the target audience as it writes directions. The goal now is to explain step by step exactly what students must do. The best directions will be simple, direct and uncomplicated.

The whole team participates in the writing and explaining of the essential question. They should also agree early on as to what the students are expected to create as a product. Finally, they should estimate how many class periods (and modules) might be required to explore the question adequately.

Once these elements are decided, much of the work can be split up and assigned to pairs, each of which will have several modules to complete. The modules do not have to be completed in a sequential manner. Pairs can begin work concurrently on several "gathering" modules, for example. One might focus on resources available over the district "intranet," while the other might focus on Internet resources.

More work is accomplished when the tasks are split up and shared across pairs.

Stage Eight - Prospecting for Good Sites

Teams will devote many hours to further prospecting - the locating of worthwhile sites and resources so that students may be directed to quality information and protected from wasteful wandering. A dozen hours spent by the teachers may save students thousands of hours and allow them to put their energy into interpretation, analysis and invention.

Stage Nine - Converting Pages into HTML

Eventually, when all of the learning activities have been outlined and described in detail, it will be necessary to convert the files of directions into well designed Web pages with proper format and good visual design.

Web pages are designed to read well on a computer screen. It is best not to overload a page with too many words in small print and best to avoid too much scrolling.

Stage Ten - Field Testing

Most research modules will require at least one major revision based on the first trial with students. Much as we might try to build a research module that successfully anticipates all problems and issues, most teams find they must adjust directions and activities in line with observations made during field testing.

Toward this end, students should be asked to make comments and suggestions to supplement the ideas generated by the invention team as they watch the unfolding of the research experience first time around.

Chapter 18 - Levels of Modules

Not all teachers are ready or inclined to plunge into a full week or more of student inquiry using new technologies.

This chapter suggests offering three levels of structured online learning experiences inspired by the two research models, **Research Modules** and **WebQuests**. While each might have its own version, they have much in common.

The idea is to offer introductory challenges (Level A) that are relatively easy, single period research tasks carefully tested and structured so that even the most hesitant teacher will find success and an immediate payoff for effort involved. Once they have been won over to this kind of thinking and learning, after 5 or 6 Level A experiences, they may move on to engage their students in more demanding research challenges (Level B) that might extend over 2-3 class periods. As comfort, competence and appetites grow, these teachers may eventually move up to the full package, advanced challenges (Level C) that are already available as "prepackaged" **Research Modules** and **WebQuests**.

Level A Challenges - Two Examples

Science

The science standards in most states call for the collection and interpretation of data. In North Carolina, for example, the standards expect the following:

Science as Inquiry - As a result of activities in grades 9 - 12, all students should develop:

Levels of Modules

- The ability to do scientific inquiry.
- Understanding about scientific inquiry.
- Abilities to perform safe and appropriate manipulation of materials, equipment, and technologies.
- Mastery of integrated process skills.
- acquiring, processing, and interpreting data.
- identifying variables and their relationships.
- designing investigations.
- experimenting.
- analyzing investigations.
- constructing hypotheses.
- formulating models.

Foul Water is an online Level A Research Module (http://questioning.org/module/fwater.html) that takes students to the EPA (Environmental Protection Agency) to explore demanding questions about acid rain data that students can download and "crunch" during a single visit to an Internet equipped lab or may be completed in a science classroom equipped with 5-8 networked computers.

Social Studies

The social studies standards in most states also call for the collection and interpretation of data. Massachusetts, for example:

Learning Standard 3: Research, Evidence, and Point of View. Students will acquire the ability to frame questions that can be answered by historical study and research; to collect, evaluate, and employ information from primary and secondary sources, and to apply it in oral and written presentations. They will understand the many kinds and uses of evidence; and by comparing competing historical narratives, they will differentiate historical fact from historical interpretation and from fiction.

What Childhood? is an online Level A Research Module (http://questioning.org/module/child.html) that takes students to the **Kids Count** Web site (http://www.aecf.org/kidscount/kc1999) funded by the Annie Casey Foundation to explore demanding questions about child-

Levels of Modules

hood in America during a single visit to an Internet equipped lab or may be completed in a social studies classroom equipped with 5-8 networked computers.

Level B Challenges – An Example

English and Language Arts

The English and language arts standards in most states call for the interpretation of literature, as was seen above with the California Standards. Students must "evaluate the structure, style, and content of the author's works."

What Digital Revolution? is an online Level B Research Module (http://questioning.org/module/digitalr.html) that takes students to a series of provocative essays about the future and asks them to figure out what techniques or devices the authors employ to make a strong case. This Level B activity would require 2-3 visits to an Internet equipped lab or may be completed in an English classroom equipped with 5-8 networked computers.

Level C Challenges

There are many online examples of these more advanced and more demanding research experiences at http://fno.org/url.html

Online References
Education Week's **Technology Counts '99** http://www.edweek.org/sreports/tc99/
Data Retrieval's Report on Readiness, "Survey Finds Teachers Unprepared for Computer Use," The **NY CyberTimes** by Pam Mendels (September 8) http://www.nytimes.com/library/tech/99/09/cyber/education/08education.html
Becker, Hank. **Teaching, Learning, and Computing** (TLC) Spring, 1998 national survey in which teachers, technology coordinators, and principals described their best instructional practices, teach-

Levels of Modules

ing philosophies, and uses of computing technologies. http://www.crito.uci.edu/TLC

Some (but not all) schools and teachers have been trying for decades to engage students in challenging research projects. The history of such efforts extends back prior to the efforts of John Dewey and more recent leaders such as Hilda Taba and John Fenton.

The best of all of these efforts always made significant use of **scaffolding** to organize and support the student investigation or inquiry, to keep students from straying too far off the path while seeking "the truth" about whatever issue, problem or question was driving the project.

The least successful efforts assumed too much about student skills, organizational abilities and commitment. Young ones were sent off on expeditions with little in the way of structure or guidance.

We should have learned by now that exploration by students progresses most effectively when those students have been well equipped, well prepared and well guided along the path. In this chapter, the focus is upon the scaffolding techniques that have proven especially worthwhile in an electronic context.

Scaffolding

Matters of Definition

What do we mean by **scaffolding** in the context of student research in school?

There is no appropriate (educational) definition in a dictionary. The term is relatively new for educators, even though the concept has been around for a long time under other names.

We tend to think of structures thrown up alongside of buildings to support workers in their skyward efforts.

"Structure" is the key word. Without clear structure and precisely stated expectations, many students are vulnerable to a kind of educational "wanderlust" that pulls them far afield.

The dilemma? How do we provide sufficient structure to keep students productive without confining them to straight jackets that destroy initiative, motivation and resourcefulness?

It is, ultimately, a balancing act. The workers cleaning the face of the Washington Monument do not confuse the scaffolding with the monument itself. The scaffolding is secondary. The building is primary.

The same is true with student research. Even though we may offer clarity and structure, the students must still conduct the research and fashion new insights. The most important work is done by the student. We simply provide the outer structure.

Characteristics of Educational Scaffolding

There are at least eight characteristics of scaffolding:

1) Scaffolding provides clear directions

Web based research units offer step-by-step directions to explain just what students must do in order to meet the expectations for the learning activity. Instructional designers try to anticipate any problems or uncertainties, writing user-friendly directions in ways that minimize confusion, place a premium on clarity and speed students toward productive learning.

The operating concept here is the "teflon lesson," a learning experience that has been well tested in advance so that anything that might go wrong is considered in advance and eliminated if possible.

We don't want our students wandering about like prospectors on the desert.

2) Scaffolding clarifies purpose

"Why are we doing this?"

Scaffolding keeps purpose and motivation in the forefront. Rather than offering up one more empty school ritual like the state report, the scaffolded lesson aspires to meaning and worth. Built around essential questions, the scaffolding helps to keep the "big picture" central and in focus.

"We are looking at this question because it is central to being human."

No "trivial pursuit" here.

Students are let in on the secret early. They are told why the problem, issue or decision is important and they are urged to care about it. They do not lapse into simple collecting or gathering. They are not caught up in mindless activity traps. Their work remains purposeful and planful. Each time they act, it is in service to the thought process, the discovery of meaning and the development of insight.

Traditional school research placed too much emphasis upon collection, while scaffolding requires continuous sorting and sifting as part of a "puzzling" process - the combining of new information with previous understandings to construct new ones. Students are adding on, extending, refining and elaborating. It is almost as if they are building a bridge from their preconceptions to a deeper, wiser, more astute view of whatever truth matters for the question or issue at hand.

Scaffolding

3) Scaffolding keeps students on task

By providing a pathway or route for the learner, the scaffolded lesson is somewhat like the guard rail of a mountain highway. The learner can exercise great personal discretion within parameters but is not in danger of "off road" stranding. Each time a student or team of students is asked to move along a path, the steps are outlined extensively. No need to wander, stray or stumble. Students may "take the curves" without fear of going over the edge.

This is more than a matter of clear directions that could just as easily be printed out on paper. The Web based lesson provides structure and guidance coincident with each step of the journey. The progression of activities is liberating yet controlling at the same time. The student moves through something like a garden, taking each Web page like flag stones. There may be more than one path wandering through the garden, but none of them leads into the jungle or a swamp or a tiger pit.

4) Scaffolding offers assessment to clarify expectations

From the very start, scaffolded lessons provide examples of quality work done by others. Right from the beginning, students are shown rubrics and standards that define excellence. In traditional school research, students were often kept in the dark until the product was completed. Without clearly stated criteria, it was difficult to know what constituted quality work.

Is it a matter of length? the number of sources cited?

Does originality count?

Does the logic and coherence of my argument matter?

What constitutes adequate evidence?

There are a dozen issues, all of which deserve attention and elaboration. As an example, consider the online rubrics for successful multimedia reports available at http://www2.ncsu.edu/ncsu/cep/midlink/rub.multi.htm

5) Scaffolding points students to worthy sources

Most educators complain that the Internet suffers from a low "signal to noise ratio" - the confusing, weak and unreliable information (noise) outweighs and threatens to drown out the information most worthy of consideration. Wary of wasting time, teachers have little tolerance for "data smog" and "Infoglut." They want to see students putting their energy into interpretation rather than wandering.

Scaffolding identifies the best sources so that students speed to signal rather than noise. Looking for the best Web sites on Columbus, Drake or Magellan to decide which would have been a better leader, the scaffolded lesson created by fifth grade teacher, Gretchen Offutt, identified 4-5 sites for each captain.

Explorer Homeport

http://wwwsil.bham.wednet.edu/Curriculum/homeport.htm

Knowing that the Web is filled with sites not worth visiting because of quality, bias or reading level concerns, the teacher visits 100+ sites per captain before winnowing the list down to 4 or 5 per captain.

Does this mean the student has no options? It depends upon the teacher. And it depends upon the school. In some cases, students must stick to the sources pre-selected by the teacher. In other cases, the student may use these sites as a starting point, extending further out into Cyberspace in search of something unusual. The scaffolding serves as an introduction, not as a corral.

6) Scaffolding reduces uncertainty, surprise and disappointment

The operating design concept for scaffolded lessons is the "teflon lesson" - no stick, no burn and no trouble. Lesson designers are expected to test each and every step in the lesson to see what might possibly go wrong. The idea is to eliminate distracting frustrations to the extent this is possible. The goal is to maximize learning and efficiency. Once the lesson is ready for trial with students, the lesson is refined at least one more time based on the new insights gained by watching students actually try the activities.

7) Scaffolding delivers efficiency

If done well, a scaffolded lesson should nearly scream with efficiency. Teachers and students should shake their heads in disbelief.

"It felt like we completed ten hours of work in just two!"

"How did we get so much done?"

This perception is achieved, in part, by virtue of comparison with the old kind of school research that was mostly about wandering and scooping. Boredom fed by irrelevance slowed the passage of time. It took forever to get the job done.

Scaffolded lessons still require hard work, but the work is so well centered on the inquiry that it seems like a potter and wheel. Little waste or wobbling. Scaffolding "distills" the work effort. Focus. Clarity. Time on task. The student is channelled. No mud flats, shoals or other navigational hazards.

8) Scaffolding creates momentum

In contrast to traditional research experiences, throughout which much of the energy was dispersed and dissipated during the wandering phases, the channelling achieved through scaffolding concentrates and directs energy in ways that actually build into momentum. It is almost like an avalanche of thoughts, accumulating insight and understanding.

In resolving the dissonance described in Chapter 4, "Students in Resonance," the work gathers speed. The drive toward meaning is accelerated. The essential question and its subsidiary questions create suction, drive, urgency and motivation. The search for understanding inspires and provokes. One loses sleep. One awakens in the middle of the night, wondering, pondering, considering.

Scaffolding

Examples of Scaffolding

Explorers' Homeport (5th grade)
http://wwwsil.bham.wednet.edu/Curriculum/homeport.htm

Fifth grade science (Planets)
http://wwwsil.bham.wednet.edu/Curriculum/paBASECAMP.HTM

Grand Prairie, Texas, Research modules
http://www.gpisd.org

Baltimore County Research modules
http://www.bcplonline.org/online

New South Wales Research modules
http://www.cap.nsw.edu.au/bb_site_intro/bbcap_intro.html

Module Maker - Offers a step-by-step method for the construction of online research modules with an emphasis upon scaffolding.
http://fromnowon.org/module/module.html

WebQuest - Offers pages describing a step-by-step method for the creation of WebQuests with an emphasis upon scaffolding.
http://edweb.sdsu.edu/webquest/webquest.html

Victorian WebQuests
http://goanna.cs.rmit.edu.au/~linpa/EPI/Conf/

Blue Web'n
http://www.kn.pacbell.com/wired/bluewebn

Chapter 20 - Modules and Standards

"This is pretty cool stuff."

Sam is not known for his enthusiasm. Especially when it comes to technology. Especially when it comes to summer workshops. He is a great history teacher, well respected and inclined toward a classical approach; but Sam has held out and dragged his heels a bit when folks pressured him to spend more time "online."

"I don't see the point." he'd grumble. "Surfing and history just don't mix. My text book is nearly five inches thick, and I just can't spare the time. The Internet is just a bunch of travel sites and pop culture. History always seem to take a back seat to current events and movies, celebrities and rock stars."

But Sam is now a convert. He has climbed on board. He has picked up the mouse. He has seen the light.

Working on a summer curriculum project aimed squarely at meeting new curriculum standards with new technologies, he has been convinced. He is building standards-based lessons that make deep use of networked information. He is proud, enthusiastic and vocal now. Once reluctant, he is now eager.

The straw that broke this camel's back?

Modules and Standards

State standards.

Once his colleagues pointed out the dramatic connection between state standards and the kinds of thinking he could promote by involving his students with electronic sources, Sam's whole attitude shifted.

"'Bout time they came up with something worth doing," he grumbled, when someone pointed out the kinds of open ended questions now asked on most state tests – all requiring inferential reasoning. They then showed him how to develop inference skills with electronic text.

"This finally makes sense to me."

Even though it is August, and Sam would normally be out playing golf or minding his grand kids at the beach, he agreed to serve on a summer invention team to develop "standards rich" learning modules for use by district teachers throughout the school year.

"We build them mean, lean and super efficient," he brags, proud of his products and the contributions of his colleagues. "It's almost as if we repackaged the Internet so that other teachers don't have to waste time."

We have growing evidence that many teachers are neither prepared nor inclined to make use of their schools' new networks. Data emerging from Education Week's **Technology Counts '99** and Data Retrieval show that some 60 per cent or more of our teachers report feeling inadequately prepared. Hank Becker's research seems to indicate that some 60 per cent or more are not especially inclined to use the new technologies with students, in part because they are concerned about the state standards and tests.

It stands to reason that we might do better enlisting the support and full participation of all teachers when we can show that networked technologies might enhance the reading, writing and thinking performance of students. We might encourage and win broader acceptance by drawing a close connection between tough state standards and technology practices emphasizing student literacy.

References

ASLA and AECT. (1998) **Information Power: Building Partnerships for Learning.** Chicago: American Library Association.

Barron, Dan. **Information Literacy: Dan's Generic Model.** University of South Carolina.

Bloom, B. (1954). **Taxonomy of Educational Objectives. Handbook I: Cognitive Domain**. New York: Longmans, Green & Co.

Brooks, M. and Brooks, J. (1993) **In Search of Understanding: the Case for Constructivist Classrooms**. Alexandria, VA: ASCD.

Bruner, Jerome. (1990) **Acts of Meaning**. Cambridge: Harvard University Press.

Culham, Ruth and Spandel, Vicki. **The Six Traits Wrting Model**. Materials available from the NWREL at http://www.nwrel.org/eval/writing/products.html

Dewey, John. (1916) **Democracy and Education**. Reprint edition, Vol 009 (October 1985,) Southern Illinois University Press.

Eberle, Bob. (1997) **SCAMPER**. Prufrock Press.

Eisenberg, M. and Berkowitz, R. (1990). **Information Problem-Solving: The Big Six Skills Approach to Library and Information Skills Instruction**. Abblex Publishing: Norwood, NJ.

Fenton, Edwin. **Teaching the New Social Studies in Secondary Schools: An Inductive Approach**.

Goodlad, J. (1984). **A Place Called School**. Hightstown, NJ: McGraw-Hill.

Henley, S. and Thompson, H. (2000) "Fostering Information Literacy: Connecting National Standards, Goals 2000 and the SCANS Report" Libraries Unlimited.

Hyman, R. (1980). "Fielding Student Questions." **Theory into Practice**; 1, pp. 38-44.

INFOZONE from the Assiniboine South School Division of Winnipeg, Canada http://www.mbnet.mb.ca/~mstimson/

Keene & Zimmerman, (1997) **Mosaic of Thought: Teaching Comprehension in a Reader's Workshop**

Langford, Linda. "Information Literacy: A Clarification" in **School Libraries Worldwide**, Volume 4, Number 1.

Learning for the Future: Developing information Services in Australian Schools (1993) Curriculum Corporation.

Loertscher, David. **The Organized Investigator** (Circular Model) California Technology Assistance Project, Region VII's web site http://ctap.fcoe.k12.ca.us/ctap/Info.Lit/infolit.html

Loertscher, David. (2000) **Taxonomies of the School Library Media Program**. San Jose: Hi Willow Research & Publishing.

McKenzie, Jamie. (1999) **How Teachers Learn Techology Best**. Bellingham, WA: FNO Press.

McKenzie, Jamieson. (1993) **Power Learning**. Newbury Park, California: Corwin Press.

NCREL (North Central Regional Educational Lab). (1995) **Plugging In.**

Pappas, Marjorie and Tepe, Ann. **Pathways to Knowledge**, Follett's Information Skills Model. http://www.pathwaysmodel.com/

Postman, Neil and Weingartner, Charles. (1969) **Teaching as a Subversive Activity.** New York: Delacorte Press.

Problems of Readiness and Preparation, The September, 1999 report of Market Data Retrieval.

Shenk, David. **(**1997**) Data Smog.** New York: Harper Edge.

Sizer, Theodore. (1984). **Horace's Compromise**. Boston: Houghton Mifflin Company.

Taba, Hilda. (1988) "A Conceptual Framework for Curriculum Design," **Curriculum: An Introduction to the Field**, ed. James R. Gress. Berkeley, CA: McCutchan Publishing Corporation, pp. 276-304.

Toffler, A. (1990). **Power Shift**. New York: Bantam Books.

Wyatt, Edward. "Encyclopedia Green; The High Road at a High Cost.," **New York Times**, October 24, 1999.

Index

Research Programs

Q

Questioning Toolkit 10, 13

R

Research Cycle 11, 63, 64, 65, 104,
      105, 110, 111, 113, 116, 143
Research modules 141, 142, 145, 146,
      151, 161

S

Sage on the stage 42
Scaffolding 155
SCAMPER 109
School research 157
Searching 19, 43, 119 81, 87, 135
Selection 69
Sherlock vi
Six Traits of Effective Writing 55
Sixty Toughest Questions 56
Sorting & Sifting Questions 24
Standards vi, 25, 40, 44, 45, 57, 99,
      133, 151, 152, 153, 158, 163, 164
Storage 69
Strategic Questions 26
Strategic Teaching 13, 54, 55, 59
Subsidiary questions 16, 65, 67, 68,
      80, 81, 82, 160
Synthesis 6, 50, 52, 64, 71, 72, 79,
      106, 133

T

Telling Questions 19, 70, 81, 120

U

Unanswerable Questions 26

V

Virginia 47

W

WebQuests 141, 151, 161

Y

Year Long Project 52